WOMEN'S BRATA RITUALS

WOMEN'S BRATA RITUALS

Sila Basak

GYAN PUBLISHING HOUSE
NEW DELHI-110002

Women's Brata Rituals
Translated by Sumanta Sen

Rs. 690

ISBN: 81-212-0897-1

Published in 2006 in India by
Gyan Publishing House
5, Ansari Road, Darya Ganj, New Delhi-110002
Phones : 23282060, 23261060
Fax : (011) 23285914
E-mail : books@gyanbooks.com
Website : www.gyanbook.com

Laser Typesetting at : Master Computers, Delhi
Printed at : Salasar Imaging System, Delhi

To my grandmothers
late Sukumari Rakshit
and
late Suruchibala Datta
whose affectionate indulgence
helped me to enquire

Contents

9. Charubala Deb Painting Lakshmi Alpana, Kishoreganj.

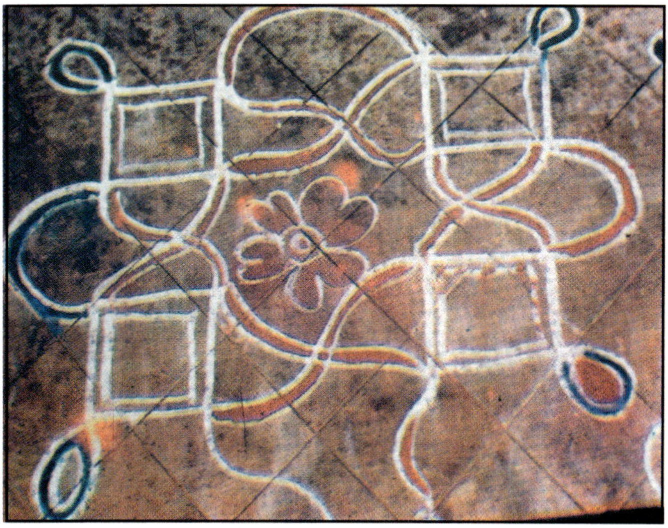

10. Gaacher Gunri Brata Alpana, Kishoreganj.

11. Pitcher used at Lakshmi Brata.

12. Alpana of Kshetra Brata.

13. Pitcher used at Meghranir Kulo Namana Brata.

14. Alpana of Shiva Ratri Brata.

15. Magh Mandal Brata—women pouring water.

16. Celebrating Magh Mandal Brata.

List of Photographs

1. Shiva Ratri Lamp, Kedua, Netrakona, Bangladesh.

2. The Manasa Motif, Artist, Nirmala Acharya, Kishoreganj, Bangladesh.

3. Pushparani Roy Painting Manasa Alpana at Bagadia, Kishoreganj, Bangladesh.

4. Manasa Brata Alpana, Kedua, Netrakona.

5. Pitcher used at Manasa Brata with artist Rabeya, Khatun, Jhikargacha, Bangladesh.

6. Nirmala Acharya Making Pitcher at Kishoreganj.

7. Sola Painting, Kishoreganj.

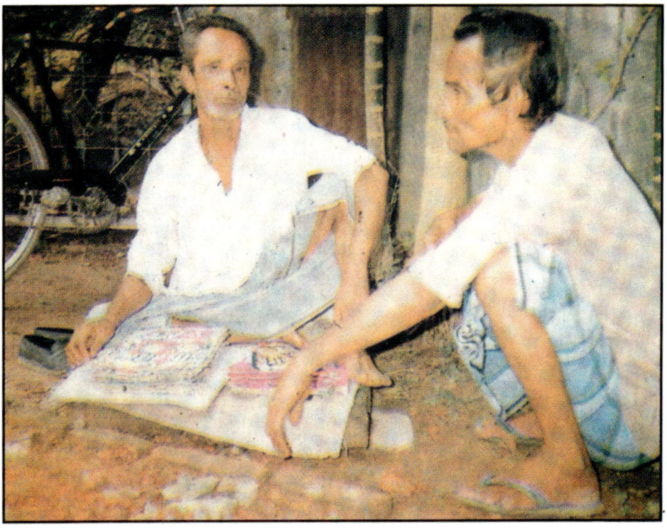

8. Sudhir Acharya Selling Ritual Paintings.

Preface

My childhood holidays used to be spent in the rural atmosphere of Murshidabad district of West Bengal. Of the things that attracted me were the various rituals performed at our home and in those of our neighbours. I used to watch with great attention every little detail and listen to the tales and rhymes. Many years later, when I began my studies in folk culture, those days came back to me and prompted me to begin my researches on *brata* in 1988.

Around this time through my family I also established contacts with Bangladesh and Orissa which helped me in my task. The book even then could not perhaps have come out but for the encouragement that I have received from many and the work on the subject done by my predecessors. While drawing from their observations I have sought to relate those with my own findings during my field surveys. The word Bengal used here does not only refer to West Bengal but also Bangladesh. Peoples of both countries have a common language—Bengali and culture of which the rural rituals are very much a part. My purpose was to show that women in the Indian sub-continent along with their counterparts in some regions of South-Asia have the same desires and aspirations, the rituals reflecting their distinct cultural milieu. The present book is not the literal translation in English of my original one in Bengali language. In the process of getting it done, certain novelties in approach and methods have added new dimension.

My travels took me to different people of India, Nepal and Bangladesh and I shall never forget their help and warm welcome that I received. I was privileged to come across many outstanding personalities of the academic world of whom I must mention the names of Prof. Ashraf Siddique, Prof. Anisuzzaman, Prof. Wakil Ahmed, Prof. Shamsuzzaman Khan, Dr. Momen Chaudhuri, Dr. Asma Begum, Mr. Ishtiaque Hasan of Bangladesh, and Prof. Pallab Sengupta, Prof. Chittaranjan Laha, Prof. Khetra Gupta, Prof. Ajitkumar Ghosh, Prof. Manas Mazumdar, Dr. Dulal Chaudhuri, Dr. Dibyojyoti Mazumdar and Sunil Chandra Basak of West Bengal. I thank them all. Here I must specially mention the name of Mohammed Saidur of Kishoreganj whose whole life is dedicated to the study of folk culture.

I shall be failing in my duty if I do not thank the authorities of Bangiya Sahitya Parishad, Asiatic Society, National Library, Bangla Academy of Dhaka for the assistance provided by them. Thanks are also due to the many others without whose support the book would not have seen the light of day.

My daughter Sudeshna (Mili) and son-in law Sumit (Joy) were the two pillars of constant support and help. The keen interest of my two nephews Parichay (Sunny) and Avinandan (Ani) provided me the encouragement to complete the book fast. I must name Shubheccha (Prince) and Rebanta (Raj)—my two grandsons, but for whose pleasant company, I could not have completed this book with satisfaction.

Sila Basak

1

Brata : Meaning and Origin

All countries have certain rites, social, or religious, which provide the variety that people seek as a relief from the humdrum routine of their daily lives. No other country, however, has so many rites and rituals as Bengal has. Bengalis seem to love these occasions which are an expression of their life-force. These rites are observed throughout the year and are associated with almost every form of activity. Bengali society has evolved through a constant inter-mingling of various cultures and this is reflected in the diverse nature of the rites.

The *brata* or the vow occupies a special place in this scenario. The *brata* is the ritual performed by women for fulfillment of desires. The rituals are performed at particular times and a particular manner and are the domestic observance of religion. At the same time they are also a continuation of the ancient belief in magic which lives even today among the tribal communities. The person who performs a *brata* is known as the *brati.*

Brata means restraint or discipline. So the observance of any *brata* is marked by a strict adherence to the rules that govern every such ritual. Behind each *brata* is the desire to get rid of the effects of sins that have been committed and earn piety. Sanyasis also observe *bratas* for attaining spiritual power to communicate with the Almighty. As Abanindranath Tagore put it, *brata* is that performed in society for getting some desired object (*Banglar Brata: Abanindranath Tagore*).

Discussing the origin of the *brata*, Niharranjan Ray has said: "The history of the *brata* is complex and goes back to very ancient times. But perhaps there can be no doubt that such performance of rituals was common even in the pre-Vedic days. Did the Aryan-Brahminic culture consider as 'brātya' (outcast) those who performed such rituals and hence the term 'brata'? It is of course difficult to establish any such relationship for want of definite evidence but such speculation may not be entirely illogical or untenable historically. The Aryans at the time of the Rg-Veda believed in the power of the yajnas and perhaps considered those to be 'brātya' who believed in the magical powers of the *brata*. It needs to be noticed that the *bratas* are more associated with lives of people in the east, like in Bihar, Bengal, Assam and Orissa. An essential feature of the observance of a *brata* is the alpana painting on the floor which is always within a circular border which speaks of an inherent belief in the powers of magic and those who believed in such powers were perhaps 'brātya' to the Aryans. (Niharranjan Ray:*Bangalir Itihas*).

On the same subject Suhrid Kumar Bhowmik has spoken of tribal traditions. He says: "The most popular chant of any Santhal *brata* is that related to the mystery of creation and the structure of the chant is the same as the ones recited at Bengali *bratas*. It starts with some person well established in society ignoring a deity. Then he undergoes a period of suffering appeals to the deity for deliverance and ultimately gets back everything with the grace of the deity. The Mangal Kavyas of Bengal are also an extension of such chants. (Suhrid Kumar Bhowmik, *Bangalir Sanskriti O Adivasi Aitihya*).

The same view, that the *brata* has its origin in tribal customs, is also held by Abanindranath Tagore. Analysing the Kulai *brata* he has spoken of cowherds masquarding as tigers and reciting rhymes because the *brata* is aimed at protecting cattle from the tigers. As Suhrid Kumar Bhowmik has pointed out, in the Santhal langauge as also in the languages of the Mundas and Kols, the word Kul means tiger and the Kulai *brata* used to be observed by the Kheroal community who worked as cowherds. With time the Kheroals got lost in the caste system of the Hindus but the Kulai *brata* remained. Similarly the Manasa *brata* has come from the Dravidian tradition. Even today some Dravidian communities worship 'manchamma' or the earth to prevent creatures underground from harming men. With Bengalis pronouncing the 'c' as 's' mancamma got transformed into 'manasa ma'. Bengali priests, however, would not agree with this as they want to relate the *brata* with the Puranas and interpret 'manasa' with Siva's 'manas kanya' or daughter born out of Siva's mind.

Speaking of the *brata* Gurubandhu Bhattacharya has said, "From time immemorial *bratas* are observed in Hindu homes and carry social and moral teachings. The chats or narration are actually a history of past prosperity. The *bratas* also reflect the ties within the family and the family's bonds with society and present pictures rich in the beauty of respect for the mother and the guru, the wife's respect for her husband and the sister's love for her brother. The words have not been fettered by the rules of grammar nor do these have any artificial decoration. The goddess is an elderly female member of the family like the aunt, ever keen to ensure peace and prosperity. She appears sometimes as the wife of a Brahmin, of a king, merchant or a milkmaid. Observed every month, the various *bratas* lend dynamism to rural life and therein lies their importance."

Performed through centuries, the non-Vedic and non-mythological *bratas* ultimately gained the acceptance of

Brahmin culture. No mention of this folk culture is to be found in the Rg-Veda or in any ancient scriptures and the Aryans had called the non-Aryans 'Anyabrata' or those belonging to a different discipline. When the Aryans performed their yajnas to Indra, these others prepared for battle and inside the houses the women observed the *brata* known as 'raṇe eo' for remaining married and not become widows after the battle. Abanindranath Tagore has quoted one of the chants:

raṇe raṇe eo raba
jane jane suo haba
akāle lakṣi haba
samaye putravati haba

will not lose husbands in battle
will be favourites of all
will bring prosperity at times of distress
bear sons when the time comes

The Aryans had called them 'anyabrati'. So when the prayer in the Shastras is for beauty (*rupam*), fame (*yas*) and wealth (*dhan*), the others prayed for crops, children, rain and the power to work. The women in the families prayed for welfare of all and so the prayers are the same. Since a *brata* is observed for the fulfillment of desire, it is not possible to separate those of the Aryans from that of the others.

The *bratas* grew from the communal life of ancient people. From the ancient tribes the Bengalis got ways to appease a cruel nature, to control the environment. The *brata* was the only means by which they thought they could protect themselves from the elements and the 'curse' of the gods. Even today the purpose of the *brata* remains the same though the characteristics have changed with the Aryan-Brahminical culture taking over. But the fact remains that the *brata* has come down from the time of the early man and his beliefs.

Fear and the urge to get over it led to the creation of an imaginery world. The advisai women feared the natural world around them and this fear led to the creation of ghosts in their minds. To keep this world at bay, to please the angry gods they worship them. The offerings to the gods are made of molasses not sugar. And of course things that are commonly grown in the region, like rice in West Bengal, wheat in Rajasthan. With time came the chants of the *bratas*, reflecting the sentiments that lay behind their observance. Surprise is one of the principal components of that sentiment, surprise caused by the planets, the moon, the sun, the tides in the rivers. The main purpose of the *bratas* is to keep the gods happy so that husbands, sons and brothers remain safe from them. Also to keep away hunger.

The uneven number dominates any *brata* and this is natural as such numbers are associated with fear. The tribals in the hoary past could not count but some things, such as three leaves of the bel tree or one of the neem, aroused questions in their minds and since they had no answer the questions led to fear. Of the even numbers, four is the most important as it signifies the four walls of a room or security.

The social life of rural Bengal is divided into various strata. At the top flies the flag of Brahminical culture and at the bottom are the backwards and the outcasts or tribals. To enter the world of these people, is to understand their minds, their customs, their culture as reflected in the various folk festivals.

That culture is also reflected in the *bratas* of today. The ancient people loved music and dancing as these helped create an imaginery world providing shelter from the harsh reality. As they danced they thought they had been able to overcome the mighty nature by the powers of their belief in magic which helped create that imaginery world. This belief lives even today among the backward people as also in the observance of the *bratas*. The same stream has ran through the ages and continues to do so.

Any discussion on the origin of the *brata* must take into account the practice of tree worship. This has come down from ancient times and is believed to be a means of satisfying an ever cruel nature. So trees like the banyan, peepul, neem, basil, are attributed divine powers and worshipped as also flowers, birds and beasts, rivers and hills. Particular deities are associated with different trees, like Siva with the bel, Sasthi with the peepul, Vishnu with basil, Lakshmi with the banana tree etc. The bamboo is worshipped as it is by the Garo tribals of Meghalaya. Some of the ingredients needed for the observance of a *brata* also bring to mind tribal customs, like the coconut, the core of the banana tree, sheaves of paddy, the signs painted on the earthen pots and the alpana with floral designs.

There are many *bratas* in Bengal which are similar to the ones observed by primitive societies for acquiring the powers of magic and fertility. With time some of these *bratas* have remained exclusively tribals and the rest have, with suitable changes, become part of Bengal's folk culture. As Abanindranath Tagore has said, "the *brata* forms the lowest layer, the base of Hindu rituals hidden deep inside the soil like a treasure trove".

Given below is a list of some of the rituals born out of primitive influence and their purpose:

Punyipukur: To bring rain.

Harir Charan: For divine blessings.

Dasputtal: For increasing powers of reproduction.

Gokal: To protect the cattle.

Guptadhan: For wealth and progeny.

Jaymangalbar: For fertility.

Savitri: For the husband's welfare.

Talnavami: For good fortune.

Itu, Asvathvanarayan: Tree worship.

Ghentu: For curing skin diseases.

Bana Durga: For taming wild animals.

Prithvi: In keeping with the earth worship in primitive societies.

Siva: For increased fertility in accordance with ancient customs.

Thoathui: Ceremony born out of faith in magic.

Tejodarpan: Same as above.

Asvathanarayan: Tree worship.

Saspata: Another form of the above.

Yachapan: Some as above.

Tara: Worship of the solar system.

Akshaytritia: Brahminic ritual born out of primitive crop worship.

Aranyasasthi: For increased fertility.

Kulkulti: Offering food, water and light to departed ancestors.

Yampukur: Water worship pertaining to ancient faith in magic.

Senjuti: For prosperity through trading in crops.

Bhratridwitia: To mark the love between brothers and sisters.

Maghmandal: Ritual relating to fertility and worship of the stars for marriages.

Panchrapuja: For cure of skin diseases.

Nakhchut: For increased beauty through herbal treatment.

Go Kshur: Worship of the cow as a mother.

Garsi: Relating to primitive deities.

Nagpanchami: Born out of Aryan-Brahmanic culture and concerns influence of primitive deities.

Kulaithakur: Same as above save for the worship of male deity.

Karam: For better crops and more fertility of the land.

These rituals make it clear that even the arrival of Hinduism could not do away with the primitive faith and whatever change took place was in terms of form. For example, there are certain directions given in Hindu religious faith about Punyipukur Brata but it had its roots in the primitive belief in certain customs which would keep away natural disasters.

A purpose of the rituals is to keep women in good health and hence the insistence on fasting during their observance and the eating of fruits and such other things. These also are a means of having some rest from their daily chores and the discipline is meant to foster faith and restrain in the women.

Now let us take a look at some *bratas* to have an idea of the socio-economic conditions in which these evolved.

Through the *bratas* the unmarried girls are prepared for the world in which they will step in after marriage, a world in which they must live in peace with their relatives. Characters from the epics are introduced in the chant as in the Dasputtal

Brata where the girl or *brati* prays for:husband like Rama, brother-in-law like Lakshman, father-in-law like Dasarath, mother-in-law like Kaushalya. As for herself she prays that she be chaste like Sita, be fortunate in her sons like Kunti, cook like Draupadi, be powerful like Durga, able to bear burdens like the Earth.

Women in the past were often forced to live with co-wives as polygamy was the order of the day. No woman liked this and harboured grudges against the other women. Thus, in the Senjuti Brata, she prays that she is able to:

> Cut the co-wife and deck her feet with the other's blood
> Burn to death all co-wives
> Cook at the co-wife's sradh (funeral feast)
> Beat the co-wife out of her mind with a broom
> Make the co-wife her maid

The girl also prays for the death of the co-wife. The best thing of course is not to have a co-wife and so she prays, *maina, maina, maina, satin yena hay na* meaning mynah, mynah, mynah please let me not have a co-wife. But if there has to be a co-wife then she should be barren, is another prayer.

Strangely enough, while it was the husband who took more than one wife, none of the prayers have any complaints against him. In fact it is always prayed that he lives like a king. Obviously life as a widow was more unbearable than one of sharing the husband with others.

In the same *brata* the girl also prays that as she worships the moon and the sun so she should be able to eat off gold plates, have bags of mohurs as also paddy and rice. It is also prayed that,

> I paint bangles of rice paste (in the alpana)
> So I may have gold bangles

Such prayers for prosperity perhaps suggest that in the past the things she prayed for were not entirely beyond her reach.

The prayers were not just for the husband's physical welfare. In an age when Farsi was the official language, she prays that her husband learns it and gets a high post in the king's court:

ārśi ārśi ārśi
āmār swāmi paḍuk fārśi

mirror, mirror, mirror
let my husband learn Farsi

Prayers also included those for sons. In the Asvathapata Brata the prayers is for 'seven sons going on seven horses' and in Harir Charan Brata it is said, 'gets a son every year and asks for a son the next year'. The woman also saw herself as being fortunate in her father and brothers. So in Senjuti Brata,

Father is emperor in Delhi
Brother has become a king

And in Punyipukur Brata,
I am the fortunate sister of seven brothers

In an age when married women had rights only over the property of their husbands and sons and none on that of their parents, the Tush Tushli Brata has chants bringing this out as also the caste division in society with the *brati* praying that after death she may be reborn in the family of a highly placed Brahmin. The *bratas* also reflect the nature of relationship between the mother-in-law and a woman (the narration in the Yampukur Brata speaks of a woman who was never allowed to observe *bratas* by her mother-in-law), between her and her sister-in-law.

The customs and superstitions that governed life in those days can be seen in the various *bratas*. For instance:

Guests must always be served and not turned away (Akshay Tritia Brata, Sivaratri and Prithvi Brata)

Cats should never be killed (Aranyasasthi Brata)

Twins will be born if two of the same fruit are eaten (Kului Mangalbar Brata)

Sinful to see the face of a barren woman or man (Jay Mangalbar Brata)

Forbidden to sleep with the head placed north (Durga Sasthi Brata)

Women should not touch conch shell, copper, cow or Brahmin during menstrual periods (Mangalchandi or Sankranti Brata)

Harmful to leave a meal half way through (Sankat Mangalchandi Brata)

Lice from the hair should not be picked on Thursday (Lakshmi Brata)

Prosperous homes cooked in cowdung fire (Ashok Sasthi Brata)

The peepul tree is holy (Asvathapata Brata)

In an age when human sacrifice was common, it was natural that this would also feature in some *bratas*, like Van Durga and Manthan Brata. The narration in the latter says:

A merchant's son had a pond dug but no water came out. The goddess Sasthi visited him in his dream and said water would come if he sacrificed the youngest son of his youngest wife. He did so, and water filled the pond.

Mercifully such *bratas* are not observed any longer.

It was an age when people believed in the supernatural, in the power of magic and this is evident from the manner of observance of some *bratas*. Like the Punyipukur, Basudhara or Kulo Namano *brata* which were observed for bringing rain. The essential purpose of *bratas*, however, was to sow the seeds of love, respect and restraint in the mind of young girls to help them grow into proper woman. To make them disciplined they were called upon to perform various *bratas* during the more cruel months.

In a caste divided society *bratas* were also observed according to caste, and community. The Kshetrathakur Brata was restricted only among the peasants. Some *bratas*, however, went on to gain wider acceptance like the Sivaratri Brata which was first observed by a member of the hunting community or a backward person. The Kukkuti Brata which has come from the Oraons of Chhotanagpur and associated with the fertility theme has now been accepted by Bengali woman desiring children.

2

Brata : Ways and Customs

In his book Religious Celebrations, Turner has said, "Rituals celebrate or commemorate trans-human power which though invisible are regarded by believers as the first and final causes of natural and cultural phenomena". Each ritual has a close and inseparable relationship with customs.

Customs are of two types, scriptural and folk. The purpose of the former is to appease the deities and supernatural forces by following certain codes laid down in the scriptures. Folk custom is the performance of rites by people in groups or individually in accordance with their own established ways, also to appease deities or evil spirits. The purpose is the fulfillment of worldly desires and the rites are performed mostly by women who have very little role in scriptural ceremonies.

Folk customs depend heavily on symbols. For instance, the alpana designs (made with rice-paste) represent the things that are desired. Such functions require considerable preparation, like selecting the site, getting the ingredients and appointing the person who will conduct the ritual. This done, the latter does the whole work himself.

In the ritual ceremonies of Bengal, there is often no place for priests or prayers, as in the *Kumari Brata*. Abanindranath

Tagore has pointed out that the whole work consists of collecting the ingredients, painting the alpana to symbolise the desired objects, the offering of flowers, recitation of chants not being an essential part of the custom.

Not all rituals are observed in the same manner. In some cases it is customary for the women to actually do what they are praying for. Like the *Saspata* ritual which is performed for a good crop. In Burdwan district of Bengal this is known as *Bhanjo,* performed in the month of *Bhadra*, the fifth in the Bengali calendar from mid-August to mid-September. The women keep soaked seeds of pulses and peas in a dish and for the next seven days water these after taking their bath, when the seeds begin to sprout, that is taken as an indication of a good harvest.

Then on a moonlit night the women gather in a courtyard with their dishes and around a raised mud platform dedicated to the rain god Indra whose symbol, the thunder, is painted on it. The dishes are kept on the platform and round it girls and grown up women (between the ages of seven and twenty five) start dancing holding each other's hands. A part of the courtyard is curtained off where sits the musician who sets the rhythm. The song that is sung is to the praise of the festival and insists that the dancing and singing is perfectly in order as this is just an annual festival. When morning comes the contents of the dishes are immersed in some pond or river.

Dance, we have seen, is often an integral part of folk ritual. There is no complex philosophy behind this, the dance is merely an expression of the joy of life. It is always a group dance, the participants being young women and girls. There are certain rituals like *Surya Brata, Kartick Brata* and *Meghranir Kulonamano Brata* in which only married women are allowed to dance. The movement is slow and anti-clockwise. In *Meghranir Kulonamano,* the women have their heads covered with the saris, holding on to the ends with their right hands and using the left to steady a winnow on their heads. They circle the place of the ritual a number of times, their feet never leaving the ground, making various movements with the upper part of the body. There is a marked difference in the dances of married women and girls. The former express physical desires through movements of the waist and front part of the body, the purpose being to please the deity of fertility. Girls on the other hand stick to normal dance movements.

These rituals of the women reflect the thoughts and concerns of a whole people and hence are important source materials for any study of the culture of ancient India.

The folk rituals lack the pomp of those of the scriptures as in most cases these are a silent communion with the deity and differences are noticed in the manner of observance from one region to another. For instance inspired by the same desire of Sun worship, there is the Amabasya *Brata* of married women in West Bengal, the Maghmandal of unmarried girls as also married women and the Chhat Puja of Bihar.

There are rituals observed exclusively by kumaris or unmarried girls, like Punyipukur, Dasputtal, Siva, Yampukur, Gokal, Basudhara etc. The close preserves of married women are many, like Itu, Savitri, Sivaratri, Santoshi Mata, Akshoy Sindoor, Madhu Sankranti etc. Those of the widows are Ambubachi, Ekadasi. Those which can be observed by all are, Janmashtami, Siva Chaturdasi, Bhaimi Ekadasi, Ram Navami, Tal Navami, Garsi.

The *brata* or the vow demands discipline in their observance and the ones for unmarried girls are aimed at preparing them for their life as housewives. Once that status is acquired, the rituals have a common purpose of ensuring that they look after the family in the desired manner.

Being a way of wish fulfillment, as beliefs go, the *brata* is always dedicated to some deity or other. The deities and some of the corresponding *bratas* are:

Sasthi: Aranya Sasthi, Jamai Sasthi, Sitala Sasthi etc.

Siva: Siva Brata, Sivaratri, Kehtrapal Brata.

Vishnu: Harir Charan, Durgastami, Anant Chaturdasi, Talnavami.

Krishna-Radha: Janmashtami, Radhashtami, Tulsi.

Indra-Varun: Punyipukur, Basudhara, Bhanjo.

Surya: Surya Brata, Maghmandal, Jitashtami (son of Sun).

Chandi: Harish Mangalchandi, Natai Mangalchandi, Bhadra Mangalchandi, Subachani Chandi.

Durga: Durgashtami, Maha Navami, Lalita Saptami, Nistarini Brata, Bana Durga.

Manasa: Manasa Brata, Nagpanchami.

Lakshmi: Bhadra Lakshmi, Kojagari Lakshmi, Kartick Lakshmi.

The Muslims as a rule do not observe such rituals but some of the Hindu *bratas* have entered Muslim society in the villages, and are jointly observed, like *Asan Pir Brata, Kanu Pir Brata, Mushkil Ashan, Asan Bibir Brata, Musafir Brata.*

The ritual, as has been seen, have often come down from primitive society. Their own *bratas* are also prayers for cure from illness, children, better crops, protection from evil spirits and natural calamities, better rainfall etc. The *Bhēnpu, Tusu, Karam Gusain, Kukkuti* are some of the Santhal and Birhor rituals, and *Barham Haar, Gauwol* are of the Ho tribes.

3

Brata : Wishes, Ingredients, Rules

The folk rituals of Bengal are always observed in a collective manner and what is desired is for the whole community. Indeed one of the purposes of the rituals is to pray for the well being of all, the woman has everybody in mind when seeking to appease the all powerful deities.

From early days, the rituals were aimed at creating consciousness about the changes in the world around, the change in seasons, the change from morning to night, life and death. Man saw these changes as bringing about many problems and complexities. He had to deal with these problems and rituals became one of the ways in which to do so. If he saw his own wrong doings, his sins as causing the problems then he had to observe the *brata* as a way of cleansing.

Women perform rites for well being and take care to ensure that all rules are being followed. Otherwise the result may be devastating. As Narayandeva's Padmapurana Kavya laments, "you lost your busband because of a faulty performance of your *brata*".

She who performs a *brata* is a *bratini* or *brati* or one who has shouldered a major responsibility. Who else but women could be entrusted with such responsibilities as the happiness of the family depended on them. From ancient times, therefore, girls have been prepared for this role in life through the many advices that lie hidden in the songs that are sung or the words that are recited at the ritual. Writing on the subject, Sister Nivedita said:

> "Great men work out knowledge and give it to the community. Thus, each civilisation becomes distinguished by its characteristic institutions. Nothing could be more perfect educationally than the *bratas* which Hindu society has preserved and hands to its children in each generation, as perfect lessons in worship, so in the practice of social relationship or in manners. Some of these *bratas*—like that which teaches the care of the cow, or the sowing of seeds or some which seem to set out on the elements of geography or astronomy—have an air of desiring to impart which we now distinguish as secular knowledge. They appear, in fact, like surviving fragments of an old educational scheme. But for the most part, they constitute a training in religious ideas and religious feeling. As such their perfection is startling. They combine practice, story game, and object with a precision that no Indian family can appreciate or enjoy as can the European familiar with modern educational speculation, India has, in these, done on the religious and social plane what Europe is trying, in the kindergarten, to do on the scientific. When we have understood the *bratas*, we cease to wonder at the delicate grace and passivity of the

oriental woman". *(Sister Nivedita: The place of the kindergarten in Indian schools : The Modern Review, August 1908).*

These *bratas* can be classified into several groups depending upon their purpose and nature. In the first place there are the ones which are essentially for unmarried or married girls. In the second category are those observed for peace in the family and for fostering good relations among the members. In the third category are the rituals from which great confidence can be derived. The fourth category has rituals meant to impart lessons in restraint among temptation while those in the fifth group are supposed to provide inspiration for doing things for general welfare.

On the subject of welfare, it needs to be understood that those observing the rituals have all living things in mind. The prayer in the *Basudhara Brata* is for rain, not only for human beings but also birds and animals. Incidentally this is a practice that was to be found in an American community also. Again if rain is desired during the height of summer then the warmth of sunshine is coveted during winter through the *Maghmandal Brata.* Always the prayer is for all living things, as also in the *Aranyasasthi Brata* where the chant expressed good wishes for the servants, cows and calves, the husband, children, waives and grandchildren. Then there is *Gokal Brata* observed for the good health of the milch cattle.

Certain couplets may create the impression that the woman is praying only for her own good, like when she says, "I beg of you that I may live happily with my husband and son". What has to be understood is that she is talking on behalf of all women. As was written in Man in India (Oct-Dec 1952), Page 214:

> "A Vrata rite to be specially called as such must be observed collectively by people having the same emotions and feelings. At least individual desires must have a collective basis. When a girl observes a rite for the growth of paddy or for rain, she observes it not for herself alone but the common desire of the community finds expression in the rites she observes. These Vrata rites are really observed for collective prosperity."

Different emotions in a woman's mind find expression through these rituals. For instance, during *Senjuti Brat* they paint designs of necklaces and bangles with rice-paste which symbolise the gold ornaments they want. The *Adar Simhasana Brata* is for getting the husband's love and its observance necessitates a grand reception to a woman who is known to enjoy that in life. Similarly ingredients also have specific purpose, the pulbul which would give elongated eyes, lac-dye and milk for a pinkish complexion, the betel-leaf for the face to be thus shaped and bananas for long and shapely fingers.

For observing these rituals or *bratas*, the women are very careful of the day, the hour, month, year, stellar positions etc. In some *bratas* the lunar calendar is followed but the general practice is to go according to the solar calendar. The *Sankranti* or the last day in a Bengali month is particularly auspicious in this regard.

There are certain things that are a must while observing rites. These are: Small earthen pitcher (ghat), mango leaf, flowers, green grass (*durba)*, paddy, lamp, basil (*tulsi*), leaves of the wood-apple tree (*bel),* drink made of the leaves of Indian hemp (*bhang, siddhi*), myrobalan (*haritaki*), sesame (*til*), curd honey, sugar, clarified butter (*ghee*), green coconut, five types of corn, betel-leaf, betel-nuts, rice, grounded rice, ears of paddy, winnow, vermilion, rice-paste, ripe bananas, clothes, handspun towel (*gamchha*), incense, small pot, earthen plates, mixture of honey, clarified butter, milk, curd and sugar (*madhuparka*), copper cup, Ganga water, a seat made of cloth, wooden seat, garland of flowers, necklace designed like the moon, fruits, wood for the altar, sticks of jute, sandalwood, sand, money, etc.

Some of these ingredients are symbols of life. The coconut and the banana symbolise fertility for they grow in clusters. The betel-leaf represents the female genital, and a water filled pitcher is seen to resemble a pregnant woman in much the same way as a green coconut does. Thus, the fertility theme plays a major role in most rituals, not surprising in an essentially agrarian society. The pitcher, the green coconut, the swastika sign painted on the pitcher can also be seen as carrying forward the traditions of a matriarchal society.

Women performing a ritual have to follow certain rules very closely. She must have a bath, put on clean clothes and not eat anything before getting down to her task. On the previous day also she should not touch any non-vegetarian food, taking mainly fruits and sweets and should practice restraint in every other way.

The performance ends with a recitation of the chant for the particular ritual. This is usually done by an elderly woman with the *bratini* (who has performed the *brata*) sitting next to her and closely following the words. When this is over, she should express her desire and touch the ground with her forehead as a mark of respect to the power that is being sought to be pleased.

The place where the ritual is being performed must be painted with alpana designs. These designs are all signs to express the desire that is being sought to be fulfilled. Each act connected with the ritual, like plucking of flowers, filling the pitcher with water, designing the alpana, is accompanied by singing appropriate songs in a chorus, the songs having come down through generations.

The *brata katha* is also a mirror of society. The tales of anger against co-wives must have been born at a time when the problem of polygamy had assumed serious proportions in a woman's life. The desire for many sons, as reflected in many of the *kathas*, reflects the premium enjoyed by male children in society and so women prayed for sons rather than daughters. Again the *brata* makes us aware of magic which is seen in all the *bratas* observed in the month of Baisakh. The *Punyipukur*, *Asvathapata* and *Prithvi* are all aimed at creating rainfall through a process of magic, namely the observance of the *brata*.

The *bratas* also show women eager not just in the welfare of their own family but that of their relations also. The faith ingredients like sheaves of corn, fish, paddy, winnow, the sun and stars to serve as the woman wants them to, also stems from belief in magic.

The *Sukla Paksha* or the bright fortnight is the most auspicious time for observing *bratas* except *Sivaratri* and those observed on the last day of the month are dependent on the solar almanac. The sun and fish found in the alpana designs represent fertility and the water filled pitcher kept in the centre of the alpana with a green coconut on top and the swastika sign on the pitcher is in keeping with the traditions of an ancient matriarchal society.

Female deities occupy the pride of place in the *bratas*. Thus, Lakshmi, Chandi, Sasthi, Manasa, enjoy greater importance than male deities like Siva, Yama, Dharma. The variety that is to be seen in the *bratas* of Bengal is not to be noticed elsewhere. Here it is worthwhile to recollect the words of Rabindranath Tagore:

> "Folk literature (the words and songs of the *brata*) has from the very beginning of life flowed down like a river and there can be no better vehicle to transport education and happiness to every home. This literature carries in it the simple ways of life in our villages and if this is allowed to die then we shall lose an important means of remembering our past". (*Preface to Paramesprasana Roy's collected work Meyeli Bratakatha or Bratakatha of Women*).

The purposes for which different *bratas* are observed can be listed as below:

1. Birth, Increased Fertility and Agricultural purposes: Punyipukur, Siva, Campa Chandan, Tilakjari, Gokal, Kulkulti, Prithvi, Asvathabat, Guptadhan, Harir Charan, Senjuti, Sandhyamani, Madhusankranti, Dasputal, Tejodarpan, Itu, Kshetra, Thoa Thui, Joymangalbar, Basudhara, Bhaduli, Itulakshmi, Yampukur, Saspata, Maghmandal, Jitashtami, Subachani, Mangalchandi. Also in some regions, Mechheni, Gudum Chuka, Aranya Sasthi, Birinchi, Bhēnpu, Bhanjo, Katyani, Karam Gossain, Surya.

2. Related to Commerce: Bhaduli, Senjuti, Suo-Duo, Nouka Puja etc.

3. Ancestor Worship: Yampukur, Kulkulti.

4. For Family's Welfare: Sivaratri, Savitri, Nakhchhut, Kulkulti, Joymangalbar, Janmashtami, Harir Charan, Sri Panchami, Soubhagya Chaturthi, Sandhyamani, Tara, Itu etc.

5. For Children's Welbeing: Sasthi, Rupasi (in Sylhet), Jitashtami.

6. For Brother's Welfare; Bhratri Dwitiya.

7. For Getting rid of Trouble: Sankata, Bipattarini, Mushkil Ashan, Samaytrani, Asan Bibi, Uddhar Bibi (Bangladesh).

8. For Cure of Diseases: Thakthaki, Jwarajwuri, Panchra Puja, Kanu Pir, Ghawa Pir, Sitala, Olaichandi, Yatali, Champak Chaturdasi, Basanta Buri, Ghentu, Ashok Sasthi, Arogya Saptami, Kamkhat, Kal Bhairab.

9. For Wealth: Lakshmi.

10. For Cattle Welfare: Gokal or Goteakshanath, Manik Pir.

11. For Inviting Rain: Punyipukur, Basudhara, Haat Ghurni, Kulo Namano, Banger Biye, Kaker Bia, Badnapota, Megharani (Bangladesh).

12. Related to Stellar World: Tara, Maghmandal, Amabasya, Purnima, Ekadasi, Maha Navami, Chandrayan, Dadhi Sankranti, Ghrita Sankranti, Aghor Chaturdasi, Akhan Dwadeshi, Troydoshi, Pashan Chaturdasi, Nrisingha etc.

13. For Recovery of Lost Things: Hajir Pir, Kalkinarayan, Dhanya Purnima.

14. Animal Worship: Gokal, Sarpa Puja etc.

15. Tree Worship: Karam, Saspata, Tulśi, Bat, Neem, Asvatha Narayan.

16. Related to Pies: Poush Sankranti.

17. For Preventing Floods: Musafir, Baghrai, Udaymangal (Bangladesh).

18. For Wish Fulfillment: Subachani, Santoshi Mata, Trinath Seva.

19. For Avoiding Boat Disaster: Khawaj Khijir, Bera Bhasano (Bangladesh).

20. For Keeping Away Crocodile: Kumir Puja.

21. For Keeping Away Tigers: Baghai, Shirni, Dakshinroy, Kulai Thakur Brata.

22. For Protection From Sorms: Paban Devata Puja, Nouka Puja (Bangladesh).

23. For Preventing Fire: Madar Bansher Jari Komai (Bangladesh).

24. Protecting Fruits and Crops from Birds: Kak Brata, Kaua Magan Brata.

25. For Attaining Heaven: Different Ekadasi, Akshoy Chaturdasi, Bhoot Chaturdasi, Nrisnigha Chaturdasi.

26. For Lineage Without Blemish: Kului Mangalchandi

27. For Husband's Love: Aadar Simhasan, Nakhchhut, Rupahalud.

28. For Husband's Love and Beauty: Adar Simhasan, Nakhchut, Soubhagya Chaturthi, Ruphalud.

29. For Removing Fear of Ghosts: Gacher Guri (Bangladesh).

30. For Performing Pious Deed: Subachani, Satyanarayan, Barkumar.

31. For Protection Against Violent Animals: Banbibi or Bandurga, Dakshinroy, Kaluroy, Baghai, Sarpapuja, Baram, Manasa.

Nagpanchami Brata's Alpana.

4

Brata : The Alpana and Rhymes

From time immemorial man has craved for beauty. First he decorated his own body. Then with the passage of time and the evolution of society, the artist in him found expression in the cave paintings, rich in artistic quality. The same craving saw the beginning of the alpana.

In India the alpana is known by different names in different states. It is 'aripan' in Bihar, 'jhunti' in Orissa, 'sathia', in Gujarat, 'rangoli' in Uttar Pradesh and Maharashtra, 'kolam' in Tamil Nadu and Kerala to name a few regional variations.

The alpana is painted on the floor of a room or the courtyard. It is rice-paste designed with fingers. Generally white, there are also coloured alpanas known as 'rangoli', the colour used being saffron, vermillion for red colour, charcoal dust for black, stems of the *siuli* flower for orange and turmeric for yellow. The alpana is a must for all auspicious occasions.

Like the name, the place designed by the alpana also varies from state to state. In South India, Orissa and Rajasthan it is painted at the entrance to the house, just outside the door, while in Maharashtra the kitchen floor is decorated. Rafiqul Alam says painting the alpana is a collective effort and professional artists are never engaged. While the artists enjoy complete freedom, certain symbols are always to be found. Also the strokes are more circular than linear. Since the expense is negligible anybody can get the alpana painted and hence it is truly a folk art.

Detailed accounts of alpana painting can be had in the Sanskrit works *Kadambari* and *Tilakmanjari*. Also in *Mymensingh Gitika* (Songs of Mymensingh) where in the *Kajallata* episode we find a girl first paints the feet of her parents, then sheaves of paddy, Shiv, Durga and their heavenly abode, Lakshmi and Narayan on lotus leaf (*edited by Dinesh Chandra Sen*).

The symbols used in alpanas seem to have come down from the ancient belief in magic, who believed in powers which would translate into reality whatever was painted. Hence a hunting scene would make the real life hunt that much easier. The paddy in the alpana symbolises a good harvest, a haystack or a pond filled with fish will actually bring in prosperity.

Brata's Alpana

The alpanas painted during the observance of any *brata*, are full of motifs pertaining to agricultural society, like ears of corn, plough, creepers, banana tree, and of course the feet and casket of Lakshmi, the goddess of wealth. While drawing her feet the women sing to the praise of the goddess reminding her that it is her blessings that keep people happy.

Abanindranath Tagore has divided the alpanas into two categories. The first are somewhat like the Egyptian hieroglyphics, a list of what is desired and therefore not art. On the other hand the different types of lotus created from imagination, the various creepers, the designs, constitute art.

While the alpana may reflect religious thoughts, essentially these are emotion. Since the emotion behind each *brata* varies so does the alpana design. The tradition goes back to the primitive ages and this shows that artistic values were always present in the folk life of Bengal. As also artistry which is evident from the alpana designs made only with some rice-paste and fingers.

In childhood man listens to rhymes and fairy tales which give his imagination a free run, as he dwells in a world of ghosts, demons, princes defeating them to rescue royal maidens. Such stories leave an imprint on his mind which remains even as he grows up but finds expression in different ways.

It is always the mother who takes a child to an imaginery world. To make him sleep, she calls upon 'Chand Mama' (uncle moon) to come down and kiss him on his forehead, or to the 'aunties of sleep' promising them lots of betel-leaves if they do their job. It is natural that the mother should do this and not the father as women are by nature more imaginative than men.

The rituals are observed mostly by women and the rhymes recited in these are like mirrors reflecting their minds. To see herself and her kind happy, the woman has always let her imagination play a part in the composition of these rhymes. Asutosh Bhattacharya has pointed out in his *Banglar Lok Sahitya* (Folk Literature of Bengal) that though these rhymes had their origin in the belief in supernatural, these have travelled far and today reflect only the desire for general welfare. The desire gets shape to the recitation of the rhymes to the accompaniment of singing and dancing. Abanindranath Tagore has also noticed an element of the theatre in the practice of cowherds dressing up one among them as a tiger and visiting homes in the village during the *Kulai Brata*.

Some of the rhymes are worth taking a look at.

(a) *Punyipukur Brata:*

"I chaste Lilabati
Fortunate sister of seven brothers,
May I die immersed in Ganga water
Watching my husband fondling my child."

(b) *Gokal Brata:*

"As I feed the cows with grass
So May I attain Heaven".
or
"As I worship and comfort my cow
So may I have golden bangles".

(c) *Asvathapata* (leaves of the pipul tree) *Brata*:

"As I bathe you Almighty Asvatha
So may my dreams come true in life".

The rhyme goes on to say that holding a green leaf of the tree will make the complexion like gold, a dry leaf will bring prosperity, a crumbling leaf will bring showers of gems and pearls, and ripe leaf will mean the woman will not be a widow in her ripe old age.

(d) *Harir Charan* (The feet of God) *Brata*: As Hari wants to know who it is who is touching his feet and what does she want, a long list is presented to him. Demands range from good looks, parents like Siva and Durga, husband like Rama, wealth decent in-laws.

(e) *Prithvi* (earth) Brata:

"Come Mother Earth, sit on the lotus,
conch-shell and wheel in hand,
Shall treat you to sweets and butter
So I may be the queen of a king."

(f) *Sandhyamani Brata:*

"She who observes this *brata*
Shall be a dister among seven brothers"

This *brata* is for life-long happiness and performed in *Vaisakh* the first month in the Bengali calendar.

(g) *Nagpanchami Brata:*

"She who turns evil into good
Lives in plenty,
She who turns good into evil
Gets burnt to ashes".

This *brata* is to keep away bad luck and snakes and is performed in the rainy month of *Sravana,* fourth in the Bengali calendar.

(h) *Natai Brata:*

"I beg in the dark and eat in the moonlight
So I get what I pray for".

Performed for general wish fulfillment.

(i) *Kulkulti Brata:* The prayer is for attaining Heaven, not just for the woman but also her parents and in-laws.

Such rhymes not only speak of a woman's desire for the welfare of all but also reflect a wide range of imagination.

(j) *Dasputtal Brata:*

Next I will be born as a human In a Brahmin clan
Next I will be born as a human Be chaste like Sita
Next I will be born as a human Got husband like Rama

So the rhyme continues expressing ten desires of the *bratini* or even more. The *brata* is observed in the month of Baisakh and ten small dolls have to be made of rice-paste.

(k) *Raṇe Eo Brata:* Observed to wish the husband success in battle. 'Ran' is battle and 'eo' means a married woman. The rhyme expresses the wish not only to remain a wife and not a widow after every battle but also to bring prosperity at times of hardship as the Goddess Lakshmi does and to be a mother when the time comes—*Samaye Putrabati Habo.*

(l) *Bhaduli Brata:*

"O river where do you go
Give (me) news of father, brother
O river where do you go
Give (me) news of husband and his father"

This *brata* used to be observed to ensure safe return of dear ones who had gone on trips by boat.

(m) *Kojagari Lakshmi Brata:*

"This *brata* removed darkness from earth.
Barren women gets son, sorrows depart

Poor gets wealth, happiness hereafter"

Observed in the month of Asvin for wealth and sons.

(n) *Garsi Brata:*

"Go away all insects
Come home mother Lakshmi"

Also observed in Asvin to invoke Lakshmi.

(o) *Maghmandal Brata:*

"Arise oh Sun, glistening all over
Worship you I do with china-rose flower

Observed in the month of Magh for getting a good husband and for the well-being of the family.

(p) *Nakhchut Brata:*

"Hair like the jute plant
Complexion like milk and lac-dye
Nose like a flute
Small feet
Face like the moon".

Observed in the month of Chaitra by married women for improved looks, husband's love and well being of children.

(q) *Tulsi Brata:*

"Basil O Basi
Speak basil of Krishna
As I hear of Krishna
I worship your feet".

The basil is considered auspicious and the *brata* is observed for the blessings of deities.

(r) *Itu Brata:*

"Itu you are my Brahmin
Itu you are Narayan
Pour water on your head
And at the final hour
Itu gives the desired thing".

Observed in Aghrayan again for happiness and prosperity.

(s) *Raldurga brata:* The rhyme speaks of a respectful homage to the sun for fulfillment of earthly desires. Observed in Aghrayan, Posh, Magh and Falgun.

Abanindranath Tagore has seen these rhymes as songs, their composition and arrangement having also a rhythmic quality which leads to dancing to their tunes. Song and drama are to be seen in the Maghmandal and Bhaduli *bratas.* (*Banglar Brata* or *Bratas* of Bengal).

There are some *bratas* which are purely female affairs and so no priests are required for their observance. The rhymes that have come up in connection with these are expressions of their innermost feelings.

5

Classification of Bratas

The *brata* which is an expression of desire can be classified first into the classical and the popular with the latter category having those which are observed by women, those by men and a third group of those observed jointly. Some *bratas* are observed by unmarried girls, some by married women, some by widows and a fourth category in which come those observed by all women.

In the classical *bratas*, priests chant slokas in Sanskrit, offerings are made to the deity and Brahmins and then the tale of the *brata* is heard. These *bratas* are: Brahmin, Baman Dwadasi, Dharma Ghat, Adar Simhasan, Tal Navami, Phal sankranti, Mishtasankranti, Solakala etc. These *bratas* are observed in accordance with the practice of sages of yore who used to worship the deities with oblations of ghee (clarified butter) for wealth, food, long life, happiness and prosperity. The observance is accompanied with a lot of show and pomp. The Adar Simhasan, for instance, starts with placing a married Brahmin woman at the centre of the alpana design and getting a female barber to attend to her toilet. At the end of the ritual she is well fed and given lots of presents including ornaments.

The observance of popular *bratas* is a much more simple affair, even though the purpose always is the same. There are some differences in the manner of observance, the popular ritual of one place may differ in the manner of observance from that in another place. For example, the Maghmandal *brata* of Bengal and Chhat *brata* of Bihar are both aimed at worshipping the Sun, the difference being in terms of style. But in all popular *bratas* the women or men (*bratini* or *brati*) directly convey their desires through silent meditation to the deity.

In Bengal more than one *brata* is observed every month. Given below is a month-wise list of some of these *bratas*:

Baisakh: Punyipukur, Akshay Tritia, Gokal, Asvathapata, Dasputtal, Adar Simhasan, Akshay Sindoor, Harir Charan. Ruphalud, Adahalud, Shankar, Jalsankranti, Guptadhan, Sandhyamani, Ghrita Sankranti, Tejdarpan, Baisakhi Purnima, Subachani, Prithvi, Sivabrata, Baisakhichampak, Darpan Sankranti.

Jaistha: Jaimangalbar, Aranya Sasthi, Sabitri Chaturdasi, Champak Chaturdasi.

Asadh: Bipattarini, Ambubachi, Kadali Sasthi, Manorath Dwitiya, Sankatmangala, Vivasvat Saptami.

Sravan: Manasa, Lunthan Sasthi, Nagpanchami.

Bhadra: Bhaduli, Janmashtami, Radhastami, Durbashtami, Talnavami, Anantchaturdasi Manthan, Sasthi-Lakshmi Puja.

Asvin: Durga Sasthi, Kojagari Lakshmi Puja, Garsi, Jitashtami, Souvagya Chaturthi.

Kartick: Yampukur, Itu, Baikuntha Chaturdasi, Bhratri Dwitiya, Durga Navami, Akashpradip, Kulakulti.

Aghrayan: Natai Chandi, Kului Mangalchandi, Raldurga, Mula Sasthi, Sejuti, Kshetra, Katyani, Itu, Thuna, Sankat Mangalbarer Katha.

Poush: Poushlakshmi, Patai Sasthi, Tush Tushli, Tara, Raldurga, Anna Sasthi, Sondar.

Magh: Sital Sasthi, Sankata Mangalchandi, Maghmandal, Raldurga, Surya, Bhaimi Ekadasi, Tribhuvan Chaturthi.

Falgun: Sivaratri, Go-Sasthi, Raldurga, Bandurga, Govinda Dwadosi.

Chaitra: Neel Sasthi, Ashok Sasthi, Ramnavami, Nakhchut, Eosankranti, Madhu Sankranti, Chaitra Lakshmi Puja, Phaldan, Baromese Subachani, Mouni Amabasya, Ghantakarna.

In addition fasts are observed on certain days of the week as part of rituals. Such as on Thursdays for Baromese Mangal Chandi and Lakshmi *brata.* On Tuesdays for Subachani, Mangal Sankranti, in different names, Jal Sankranti, on Saturday for Santoshi Ma and on full moon and moonless nights. These *bratas* are observed essentially by girls and women though some are observed by men also. Since girls are by nature more imaginative and married women more practical, there are certain differences in the ways they observe their rituals.

The *bratas* observed solely by unmarried girls are: Punyipukur, Prithvi, Dasputtal, Siva, Champak, Yampukur, Asvathapata, Manorath, Sejuti, Bhatridwitiya, Tus Tusli, Gokal, Maghmandal, Basudhara, Sandhyamani, Harir Charan, Jaymangalbar.

Married women observe a far larger number of *bratas.* These are: Eosankranti, Jaymangalchandi, Kului Mangalchandi, Sankat Mangalchandi, Aranya Sasthi, Am Sasthi, Lotan Sasthi, Durga Sasthi, Gostha Sasthi, Ashok Sasthi, Guptadhan, Nitya Sindoor, Akshay Sindoor, Akshay Phal, Akshay Ghat, Madhu Sankranti, Ghrita Sankranti, Darpan Sankranti, Adahalud, Ruphalud, Adar Simhasan, Misti Purnima, Padma Purnima, Baisakhi Purnima, Savitri, Saubhagya Chaturthi, Nakhchut, Itu, Kshetra, Jvarajari, Jal Sankranti, Sivaratri, Santoshi Mata, Nagpanchami, Baisakhi-Champak etc.

Widows also observe some *bratas* like *Ambubachi* and *Ekadasi.* The former involves the cooking of food for three days just before the seventh day of Asadh. From Asadh 7, no fire is lit for three days and the widows take milk that has not been heated, fruits, sago etc. The idea is that these three days constitute the menstrual period of Earth and so stern discipline must be maintained then. The land is not ploughed, it is not even dug for any purpose and no seed is sown. The *brata* has similarities with the *Karam* of tribals and the *Rajah Sankranti brata* of Orissa.

There are also *bratas* observed by men, such as Karmapurus, Kalkinarayan, Nagpanchami, Siva Chaturdasi, Janmastami, Akshaytritia, Satyanarayan, Harir Mangalchandi. The tale or katha of Siva Chaturdasi informs that this was first observed by a hunter. In the Contai area of Midnapore district the day after Kali Puja is observed by both men and women as *Darpan Darsan*, when barbers show reflections of people's faces on their mirrors and collect clothes and money the belief being that this brings back memories of childhood and increases longevity. In Birbhum, Burdwan and Hooghly districts men observe Mangalchandi *brata* and Bhanjo in Murshidabad and Birbhum. In Bangladesh also men observe *bratas* such as Kalkinarayan, Siva Chaturdasi, Janmashtami, Karmapurus etc. Also the help and cooperation of men is required in the *brata* observed by girls and woman and sometimes they also participate in these. Some such *bratas* are, Siva Chaturdasi, Dadhisankranti, Janmastami, Radhastami, Satyanarayan, Itu, Akshaytritia.

Earlier mention has been made of *bratas* observed solely by unmarried, girls, married woman and widows. But, that does not me^n that they do not jointly observe any of these rituals.

Some of the classical *bratas* are observed according to planetary position, such as Sivaratri, Purnima, Amabasya, Mahanavami, Budhashtami etc. Here the Brahmin influence is noticable though some of these reflect tribal customs in a refined manner. The *bratas* which are essentially tribal are:

Ho: Baram Har, Gauol, Oagotra, Bonga.

Santhal, Birhor: Bhēnpu, Tusu, Karam, Kukkuti.

The tribals of Chittagong in the Rangamati area observe *Nabavarsa* and those of Mayurbhanj in Orissa observe *Akhandashikar, Bandona, Damodar.* The purpose is always to cure diseases, ward off evil influence and for increased production in the fields.

Different *bratas* have to be observed for different deities. Most of them have the power to cause harm and so have to be kept appeased for peace and well being as otherwise they would destroy everything. The deities take on human forms and behave like them as is seen in the tales of the *bratas.* Given below is a list of the *bratas* devoted to different deities:

Sasthi: Jamaisasthi, Lunthansasthi, Dhulasasthi, Bodhansasthi. Mulasasthi, Sitalasasthi, Ashoksasthi, Vivahasasthi, Jalasasthi, Go-sasthi, Annasasthi, Krishnasasthi, Chandanisasthi, Manthansasthi.

Siva: Sivaratri, Kshetrapal *brata*, Siva *brata.*

Vishnu: Harir Charan, Durgashtami, Anant Chaturdasi, Talnavami.

Krishna-Radha: Janmashtami, Radhasashtami, Tulsi.

Indra-Varuna: Punyipukur, Basudhara, Bhanjo.

Surya: Surya *brata*, Maghmandal, Jitashtami, Chungir *brata*, Itu, Ashta Lokpal.

Chandi: Haris Mangalchandi, Nataimangalchandi, Sankat Mangalchandi, Kului Mangalchandi, Bhadra Mangalchandi, Nikat Mangalchandi, Bhauta Mangalchandi, Jaymangalchanir, Subachanichandi.

Durga: Durgashtami, Mahanavami, Lalita Saptami, Bipattarini, Mangal Sankranti, Bandurga, Subachani, Nistarini.

Manasa: Manasa *brata*, Nagpanchami.

Lakshmi: Bhadralakshmi, Kojagari Lakshmi, Pous Lakshmi, Chite Lakshmi, Kartikeya Lakshmi, Barlakshmi.

Lakshmi: Bhadralakshmi, Kojagari Lakshmi, Pous Lakshmi, Chite Lakshmi, Kartikeya Lakshmi, Barlakshmi.

Yama on his carrier, the buffalo.

The practice of observing *bratas* is not restricted to Hindus only. Muslims also have their *bratas* such as, Hajir Pir *brata*, Khawaj Pir *brata*, Madar Banser Jari *brata*. Also there are some observed by both communities jointly, like, Asan Pir *brata*, Kanu Pir *brata*, Mushkil Asan, Ghawa Pir *brata*, Satya Pir *brata*, Kuloghat, Asan Bibir *brata*, Musafir *brata*. These have been retained by Muslims even after conversion to Islam sometimes with changes in the name. Thus, the *Satyanarayan* of Hindus has become *Satyapir* of the Muslims. In various parts of

Bangladesh both Hindus and Muslims perform the *Go Brata* for the welfare of cattle.

People irrespective of religion share the same concerns and desire. To escape the wrath of Agni the fire god, Muslims of Bangladesh observe *Madar Banser Jari* in the month of Magh on the full moon night. The *Hajir Pir brata* is observed to get back lost things and the *Asan Pirer brata* is observed by women of both communities for the safe return of husbands who have gone on trips by boat, a common feature of life in riverine Bangladesh. For curing ailments *Kanu Pir brata* is observed at Kishoreganj by both unmarried girls and married women.

6

Brata : Folk Tales

An essential part of folk culture is the folk tale. It is a tale which gains circulation by word of mouth both among the learned and the illiterate. Though a folk tale does not discuss anything that is fundamental, it has a liveliness that helps it transcend geographic barrier. In the case of Bengalis of West Bengal and Bangladesh this, however, could never be a problem as both people share a common culture. A feature of such tales is that here the guilty never gets away, is always punished.

Folk tales can be divided into fairy tales, animal stories, legends, stories in ballads and of course the *brata katha* or the narration at rituals.

In animal stories or fables, the characters are of course not human but they speak our language, behave like us. Small in size, there is always a moral at the end of each story, the animals symbolising the ways, the aspirations, the lowliness, the courage, of the human world. Anthropologists insist that these are the oldest forms of folk literature.

Fairy tales are to be found in every country save those in the African continent. Largest in size, in these tales it is imagination which reigns supreme, kings, queens, their courtiers and servants co-existing with supernatural beings like demons, ghosts, fairies and witches. There are also imagined animals like horses with wings, talking birds together with the actual ones. A fairy tale always has a happy ending in keeping with the inherent desire in every human being for happiness. Fate plays an important hand in any fairy tale.

The *Loka Purana* or Myth is what earliest man had created in his mind that had not yet been fully developed. These are set in heaven, earth, and the netherworld. Such stories have a strong religious content and also offer fantasy a free run. It is seen that myths are to be found more among communities which are more stable than the others and also have strong links with the past. The myth is the basis of all great Epics like the Ramayana, the Mahabharata, the Illiad or the Odyssey. Myths abound among the tribals of Bengal but not in the Bengali community whose mythological tales have grown up around certain deities like the Sun god, Manasa, Gorakshanath, Sitala and Kalyaneswari.

The tales of the ballads, or *Gitika*, are very popular because of their dramatic quality. These are fast paced, racing towards the denouement, carrying in them the pains of separation, the desire to be united, success and failure. In Bengal the tales of *Purba Banga Gitika* and *Mymensingh Gitika* are highly popular. In these women are the principal characters and social sanction has been given to their right to free love. Dinesh Chandra Sen has said, "The loves of heroines like Mahua and Malua is comparable to that of Sakuntala, Malavika and Urbashi" (*Dinesh Chandra Sen* : *Brihat Banga*, Calcutta, 1934).

The legend begins where history ends. These are a spicing up of tales from the hoary past with some folk belief and the introduction of some historical character and place. These are not fairy tales in that people believe these.

Brata Katha or the narration during the observance of a ritual has close relationship with beliefs that have come down through the ages. The narration always ends in the characters getting rid of their troubles through divine intervention. The features of such narration are, highlighting the glory of the deities, tolerance of women and their service towards mankind, the dominance of the powers of magic, woman's love for her children etc.

The stories of the *Brata Kathas* can be compared to the fairy tales in that in both the characters achieve mission or get what they strongly desire, like children for a childless couple. The deities of course play the central role in the *Kathas* unlike in the fairy tales. For instance, in a fairy tale the prince can himself defeat the demons to rescue his princess, in the *Brata Katha* it is the deity who does the job. In some cases the fairy tales are suitably changed to serve the purpose of a *Brata katha.* An example of this can be had in the *Brata Katha* of Sankata.

There was a king who had seven queens, none of whom had given birth to children. This made the king unhappy as also his wives. One morning the king got up and found the courtyard had not been swept. He called for his *kotowal* (police chief) and ordered him to bring the sweeper. The *kotowal* went to the sweeper's house and found him having his meal. The *kotowal* said, "how is it that you have sat down to eat without sweeping the palace courtyard"? The sweeper answered, "Sir, I will speak the truth if you promise not to scold or punish me". The *kotowal* assured him that he had nothing to fear and the sweeper said, "Sir, if I see the face of that king without children in the morning then my whole day is spoiled and I cannot eat anything. So today I decided to first eat and then go to the palace to do my work". On hearing this the astonished *kotowal* returned and told the king what he had heard. The words saddened the king who said, "from today I shall not show this cursed face to anybody" and went to his bedroom.

At this time a sanyasi arrived and called for the king. He came out, paid respects to the sanyasi and took him to his court. On the way the sanyasi said, "King why are you so worried? I know all about your problem and you need not feel dejected. I have here a medicine which if fed to your queens will make them give birth to children. But you must promise one thing. Of the seven sons that will be born, you will have to hand over to me the one that is the most handsome". The king agreed, thinking that if seven sons were born he would have no problems handing over one.

The sanyasi departed and the king told his wives to share the medicine among themselves. Now the king loved his youngest queen the most and so the six others shared the medicine among themselves leaving nothing for the youngest. When she came and asked for her share, they told her that by mistake they had left nothing for her but she need not worry. The medicine had been grinded into paste and if she washed the grinding stone and drank the water it would have the same effect. In her innocence the youngest queen did as she was told.

The queens got pregnant and after ten months delivered. The first six queens delivered sons but none was normal. One was blind, one lame, another a dwarf and such others and the youngest delivered a conch shell. The king said, "at least the first six have delivered human beings no matter how deformed but what is this that the youngest has done"? He discarded her and the poor queen left with her conch shell, built a hut and began living in it.

Days passed and the conch shell grew in size. At night in her sleep the queen could feel somebody suckling her breast, but on waking up she would see nothing. One night she pretended she was asleep and saw a child coming out of the shell. Delighted, she grabbed the child, said "now I won't let you go" and broke the shell. At this the child said, "what have you done mother, now the sanyasi will come and take me away". The queen, however, paid no heed to his words. Absolutely delighted to hear him address her as mother, she decided to take him to the palace in the morning and show him to the king.

In the morning she offered prayers to the deity Mangalchandi and went to the palace with her son. The king was equally delighted. He listened to the queen's story, apologised for his earlier behaviour and assured her that none would be able to take the son away from them. They began to live happily together.

Twelve years passed. Then one day the sanyasi reappeared. Seeing him the king was frightened. The sanyasi said, "Well king where are your sons? I hope you remember your promise"? The king replied that he did remember but only six queens had delivered sons and a conch shell was born to the seventh. The sanyasi said that he wanted to see the children and they were brought. Seeing them, the sanyasi said, "You can hardly call these deformed creatures son, where is my Sankhanath Buteswar?" Saying this he blew on a conch shell and called out "where is Sankhanath Buteswar" which caused the young prince to come out. The sanyasi told the king, "why did you hide him while showing those others" and left with the boy.

Unable to do anything out of fear, the king silently shed tears and the youngest queen began to cry. Other women to the neighbourhood gathered round her and one of them, an old woman, advised her to observe the Sankata Brata as that would bring back her son. The queen eagerly asked what she would have to do and the old woman told her. On a Friday she fasted and spent the whole day praying to Sankata, not for a moment allowing her attention to waver.

Meanwhile after travelling some distance the sanyasi asked Sankhanath whether he would take the straight road or a roundabout way, which was shorter but through land infested with wild animals. The lad replied, "I am a king's son, I fear none and so I will take the roundabout way". This pleased sanyasi as he saw in the lad a fit sacrifice for the goddess. He took him to a dense forest.

In the forest Sankhanath saw a Kali temple. He paid his respects to the deity and then entered a hut with the sanyasi. The latter took him for a bath after which he told Sankhanath to wait while he performed puja and warned him not to open the door facing south. Then he went out to perform the puja.

His warning made Sankhanath curious about that door. Quietly he opened it and was stunned by what he saw. There was a pond, the water red as blood in which floated like lotuses several severed heads which began laughing on seeing him. Sankhanath wanted to know who they were and why they were laughing. They replied that they had also been princes who had been sacrificed by the sanyasi to the deity as he would Sankhanath. The lad wanted to know whether there was any way in which he could escape death and the heads said they would tell him if he saved them. Sankhanath agreed to do so.

They said, "When the sanyasi want you to lie prostrate in front of the deity, tell him you do not know how as you are a prince, and so you would have to be shown. Then the sanyasi will lie prostrate and at that moment you must cut off his head. Then sprinkle the blood and the flowers you will see in the temple on us and we shall return to life." Sankhanath assured them that he would and told, shut the door and sat down to meditate.

The sanyasi meanwhile was in great spirits. He had offered to the deity 107 and how only one remained. Hurriedly he finished his puja, skipping over some of the rites which displeased the goddess. Then he took the prince to the temple and asked him to worship the goddess by lying prostrate after which he would be given things to eat. Sankhanath did as he had been told, asked the sanyasi to show him and as the latter lay down severed his head. Then he paid respects to the deity, gathered the flowers and blood and sprinkled these on the severed heads. Immediately they returned to life and began thanking him. News of his deed spread and the local king, happy that the sanyasi was dead, took him to his palace. When he came to know who Sankhanath was he gave his daughter in marriage to him and sent the two to Sankhanath's father's kingdom.

When Sankhanath and his bride reached the kingdom, the king, his father, was mightily pleased and called for all the queens. That Friday the youngest queen had just finished her prayers when her maid informed that her son had returned and with a wife. The queen crying in happiness and all the seven queens took the young bride inside. The princes whom Sankhanath had saved had accompanied him and the king thanked them for saving his son. Then arrived the old woman who was also thanked for telling the queen to worship Sankata. The king then ordered that all in his kingdom must worship Sankata and told the other princess that on their return to their kingdoms they must also issue similar orders as it was Sankata who had saved them also.

This is a wonderful fairy tale. It has also the motifs to be expected in such a tale. There is the king without children, his seven queens, their sorrow, the use of magic to make them pregnant, the jealousy of the older six, the birth of the conch shell, severed heads which can speak and the ultimate happy ending. Deities do not feature in it in a big way except at the end when the king orders the worship of Sankata.

Like fairy tales, animal tales have also found place in the Brata Katha, accompanied with rituals that need to be performed. As these kathas are aimed at fulfilling a definite purpose, the characters which feature do not enjoy any variation and thus at times somewhat boring.

An important brata in the Jhargram area of West Bengal is the Karam Brata in this adivasi dominated region, the Hindu deity Karam Thakur is worshipped as the deity of agriculture. The Brata Katha is as follows:

There was a merchant who had twin sons, Karam and Dharam. When they grew up Bharam set out for the purpose of trading. He took with him a bull to carry his sack of merchandise. Karam remained in the village to look after their landed property as their father had died. Days and months passed but Dharam did not return. The time came for the worship of Karam Thakur in the months of Bhadra and a sad Karam realised he would have to perform the ceremony without his brother.

Karam, whom the villagers called Karma, brought branches of trees from the nearby forest and planted these in his courtyard around which he organized singing and dancing.

At this time Dharam returned, his sack full of gems. At the entrance to the village he was told that his brother had given up farming and spent all his time worshipping the branch of Karam tree, drinking and dancing. Dharam did not like this, particularly as his wealth had made him proud and haughty. Leaving his bull behind he ran to his house and found Karam doing exactly as he had been told.

Mad with anger Dharam uprooted the branch and kicked away the ingredients of the worship. Then when his anger subsided he remembered his bull and the sack of gems. He went to look for it but the bull was not to be found. After a long search he returned to where their home was to discover that nothing existed, the huge house, cattle, everything had disappeared. Only Karam lay on the ground weeping. Because of Dharam's sin they had lost everything as Karam Raja deserted them. Ultimately they decided that they would have to live as labourers.

The two brothers went to a distant village to work on the fields of a farmer. At noon the farmer came with *muri* (puffed rice) for the labourers but tired though they were, the brothers felt shy of taking their share as after all they had also been landowners only the other day. So they went hungry. At the end of the day the others got their wages but the farmer told the brothers to come the next day. This angered the brothers and they decided that at night they would pluck the paddy they had sown. That was what they did but were surprised when the uprooted paddy straightened and got planted again.

Next day the brothers went to another village. There also they found work but again when the time for payment came they were asked to return the next day. They returned home and together with their wives began to curse their ill luck. Ultimately Karam said, "brother Karam Raja is against us and so nothing will come our way. I will go and search for him to beg his forgiveness and bring him back". Dharam said he would also go but Karam stopped him saying that he should instead look after the ruined house. He then set out not knowing where he would find the deity.

With only a *gamcha* (homespun towel) round his waist, Karam walked for miles till he came to a pond. He went to it to quench his thirst but found it dry. Karam struck his forehead and wailed, "On Karam Raja am I to be denied water also". The pond said, "Who are you and why have you taken the name of Karam Raja"? Karam told his story, leaving out nothing.

Hearing him, the pond said, "If you meet Karam Raja please ask him why I have gone dry, what sin I had committed and where lies my salvation".

Promising to do so, Karam resumed his journey. At one place he saw many cows grazing on a field. He thought he would drink some milk but the cows attacked him. In desperation he again took the name of Karam Raja at which the leader of the herd wanted to know why he did so. On hearing Karam's story the leader said, "If you meet him ask him why we are suffering like this. We have no shed to live in, no cowherd to look after us."

Karam said he would do so and began walking again. When his feet were about to collapse, he saw horses with shining backs. He thought if he could get on one then he would not have to walk. But here also luck was not with him as the horses almost trampled him to death. Again he cried out the name of Karam Raja, beseeching him to save him. At this one of the horses asked, "What is this, do you know Karam Raja"? Again Karma had to tell his story and the horse said, "If you meet him find out what we must do to get riders and owners". Karma agreed to do so.

Next Karam came to a village where he met two girls, one of whom could not left her foot from the husking pedal and the other could not bring her hand out of the pan in which she was frying chura. Like the pond, the cows, the horses they also wanted him to find out from Karam Raja what they must do to free themselves. Next he met an old man who wanted him to know from Karam Raja how he could get rid of the bundle of thorns on his head. Similar requests were made by a huge python lying immobile on the road and who wanted to know how he could move and also a fig tree whose question to Karam Raja was why were his fruits filled with insects and inedible.

Crossing many rivers and hills, Karam at last reached the sea. There he sat on the shore wondering how he would cross when he saw a crocodile, fierce in appearance. Out of fright he shouted, asking Karam Raja to save him. The crocodile, however, said he would take Karam across the sea on his back but he must find out from Karam Raja why he had to keep on floating and not go below water even for a second. Karam was still scared but with no other way out, got on the back of the crocodile.

Thus, he travelled for many days and nights. When at last he reached the coast it was morning and there in a hole he found Karam Raja. He went forward and was aghat to find the hole filled with excreta. The deity was satisfied, the excreta disappeared and Karam Raja said, "What can I do for you"?

"Lord I want nothing, I just want to take you back", replied Karam.

"Why should I go, Dharam had plucked me out and thrown me away"., replied the deity in mock anger.

"If you don't come then I shall lay down my life here", said Karam.

Karam Raja then said, "Alright but I won't go with you. Return, make arrangements for my worship and I shall arrived in the month of Bhadra when the moon is up". He then gave food to Karam who, without realising it, had starved for the last twelve years. Karam was about to return when he remembered all that had happened on his way and wanted the various answers as he had been asked to do. Karam Raja provided the answers.

The crocodile was waiting. He wanted to know his answer but Karam said he must be taken to the other shore first. When he reached Karam told him that if he could give the ornaments he had swallowed with those wearing those, to some good Brahmin then he would be able to go under water. The crocodile agreed but said since he knew no Brahmin Karam would have to take the ornaments. Then he threw these out.

Then he met the fig tree and said his fruits would become edible if he gave to some good Brahmin the pot of money that lay below his roots. The tree agreed but said Karam must take the pot with him. Karam dug it out and found the fruits now tasted nice. The python also had swallowed a lot of ornaments which he had to vomit out and these also went to Karam. The old man with the bundle of thorns was a miser and he got rid of his misery by giving his stored wealth to Karam. The two girls also had saved money which went to Karam, the lead horse accepted Karam as his master and of the others as did the cows whom he met next. As for the pond, it was filled with water once four copper vessels full of money were dug out of four corners and donated to a good Brahmin who was Karam himself.

This way the two brothers got back everything and on the appointed day the deity was worshipped with pomp and splendour.

When the brata is observed this story is narrated and the offerings include, water, figs, clay horses etc. Though the brata had its origin among the Oraon and Munda tribals, today it has spread among Hindus also and is another example of many Hindu rites owing their origin to pre-Vedic days.

The Karam tale has a lot of similarity with a Santhali tale. It was first recorded in Santhali language by P.O. Boding in his *Folklore of the Santal Parganas* and later translated into English by Cecil Henry Bompas. The translation runs as follows:

Karmu and Dharmu

There were once two brothers Karmu and Dharmu. Karmu was a farmer and Dharmu was a trader. Once when Dharmu was away from home Karmu gave a religious feast and did not invite Dharmu's household; when Dharmu returned and learnt this, he told his wife that he also would perform the ceremonies in his house, so they set to work and were employed in cooking rice and vegetables far into the night; and Karam Gosain came down to see what preparations Dharmu was making in his honour, and he watched from the back of the house.

Just then Dharmu strained off the water from the cooked rice and threw it out of the window, and it fell on Karam Gosain and scalded him, and as the flies and insects worried the wound, Karam Gosain went off to the Ganges and buried himself in the middle of the stream. As he had thus offended Karam Gosain, all Dharmu's undertakings failed and he fell into deep poverty, and had not even enough to eat, so he had to take service with his brother Karmu. When the time for transplanting the rice came, Dharmu used to plough and dig the ditches and mend the gaps along with the day labourers. Karmu told him not to work himself but act as overseer of the other labourers, and the labourers also told him that it was not suitable for him to work as a labourer himself, but Dharmu said that he must earn his wages and insisted on working; and in the same way Dharmu's wife might have acted as overseer of the women, but she was ashamed not to work too.

One day they were transplanting the rice and Karmu brought out breakfast for the labourers; he told Dharmu and his wife to wash their hands and come and eat; but they answered that they belonged to the household and that the hired labourers should be fed first, so the labourers ate and they ate up all the rice and there was nothing left for Dharmu and his wife. When the midday meal was brought the same thing happened, Dharmu and his wife got nothing; but they hoped that it would be made up to them when the wages were paid, and worked on fasting. At evening when they came to pay the wages in kind, Dharmu's name was called out first, but he told his brother to pay the labourers first, and in doing this the paddy as all used up and there was nothing left for Dharmu and his wife; so they went home sorrowfully, and their children cried for food and they had nothing to give them. In the night Dharmu's wife said "They promised to pay us for merely looking after the work and instead we worked hard and have still got nothing. We will not work for them anymore; come, let us undo the work we did today, you cut down the embankments you repaired, and I will uproot the seedlings which I planted." So they went out into the night to do this. But whenever Dharmu raised his spade a voice called out "Hold, hold!" And whenever his wife put out her hand to pull up the rice a voice called out "Hold, hold!" Then they said "Who are you who stop us?" And the voice answered. "You have done evil and offended Karam Gosain by scalding him; this is why you have become poor and to-day have worked without food and without wages; he has gone to the Ganges and you must go and propitiate him. And they asked how they should propitiate him. And the voice said "Grind turmeric and put it on a plate, and buy new cloth and dye it with turmeric and make ready oil, and take these things to the Ganges and call on Karam Gosain." And they believed the voice and the next day did as it commanded, and set off, leaving their children in charge of Karmu. On the way they came to a fig-tree full of figs and they went to cat the fruit; but when they got near they found that all the figs were full of grubs, and they sang :

> "Exhausted by hunger we came to a fig-tree,
> And found it full of grubs,
> O Karam Gosain, how far off are you?"

Then they came to a mango tree and the same thing happened. And they went on and saw a cow with a calf; and they thought that they would milk the cow and drink the milk, but when they went to catch it, it ran away from them and would not let itself be caught; and they sang : -

"We go to catch the cow and it runs away,
We go to catch the calf and it runs away,
O Karam Gosain how far off are you?"

But the cow said to them—"Go to the banks of the Ganges. Then they came to a buffalo and went to milk it, but it lowered its head and charged them; and Dharmu cried but his wife said "Don't cry" and sang.

"If you go to catch the buffalo, Dharmu,
It will kill you.
How shall we drink milk? How shall we drink milk?"
How far of are you, O our Karam Gosain?"

And the buffalo said "Go on to the bank of the Ganges." Then they came to a horse and they thought that they would catch it and mount it, but it kicked and snorted; and they sang:—

"Dharmu tries to catch the horse:
But it kicks and runs away.
How shall we reach the Ganges?
O Karam Gosain, how far off are you?"

And the horse said "Go to the banks of the Ganges." Then they saw an elephant but it would not let them approach, so they decided to push on straight for the river, and they saw under a banyan tree a large pot full of rupees, but they were so disheartened that they made no attempt to touch it; then they met a woman who asked where they were going and when she heard, she said "For twelve years I have had a *pai* measure stuck on my throat; ask Karam Gosain for me how I am to get rid of it," and they promised; and going on they met a woman with a bundle of thatching grass stuck to her head; and she made them promise to ask Karam Gosain how she could be freed; then they met a woman with both her feet burning in a fire and another with a stool stuck fast to her back and they promised to enquire how these might be delivered.

So at last they came to the Ganges and they stood on the bank and called to Karam Gosain ; and when he came they caught hold of him and he said "Fie, what low caste person is touching me?" But they said, "It is no low caste person, but Dharmu." Then they bathed him and anointed him with oil and turmeric and wrapped him in the new cloth which they had brought, and thus they persuaded him to return; so they rose up to go back, and Dharmu asked about the women whom they had met, and Karam Gosain said: "The woman has a stool stuck to her back because when visitors came she never offered them a seat, let her do so in future, and she will be freed; and the woman has her feet burning in the fire because she pushed the fuel into the fire with her foot; let her not do so in future, and she will be freed; and the woman has the thatching grass stuck to her head because when she saw a friend with straw sticking in her hair she did not tell her about it; let her do so in future and she will be freed; and the woman has the pai measure stuck to her throat because, when her neighbour wanted to borrow her measure, she would not lend it; let her do so in future and she will be freed." And Karam Gosain asked whether they had seen an elephant and a horse and a buffalo and a cow and money and mangoes and figs and Dharmu said "Yes," but that he had not been able to catch the animals and the fruit was bad. Karam Gosain promised them that on their way back they should take possession of all; and they did so and mounted on the elephant and returned to their home with great wealth. On their way they met the four women and told them how they could be saved from their troubles. The villagers welcomed

Dharmu and he arranged a great feast and gave paddy to all the villagers to husk; but when they had boiled it the weather became cloudy so that they could not dry it, so they prayed to the sun and he at once shone out and dried the paddy.

Then a day was fixed and they prepared rice beer, and worshipped Karam Gosain and they danced all night and got drunk and enjoyed themselves, [Cecil Henry Bompus : *Folklore of the Santal Parganas* (1981), pp. 32-36].

In this tale is to be found all the elements of folk tales. The merchant was rich and had everything, one of his sons had earned wealth through commerce and the other had prospered as a farmer. But then fate struck a cruel blow because of Dharam's fault and this is so often to be found in folk tales.

Then Karam went through many trials and tribulations to satisfy the deity and earn back all that had been lost. Here we have the elements of both fate and opportunity.

The element of surprise is essential in such a tale. The surprises are provided by the stories of the pond, the cows, horses, old man with the burden, the two girls and the crocodile. And then there is magic as witnessed in the manner in which all problems were solved.

Prithvi Brata

Observed all over West Bengal, particularly in the border areas in the west, and is related to the belief that rain can be brought down by magic to help agriculture, and thus inherent in it is the primitive faith in the power of magic. The tale of the brata is as follows:

A bania named Narahari lived in Hariharpur. He had two wives, Lakshmi and Saraswati. Two years after he married Saraswati gave birth to a son and so became the favourite wife of Narahari. This made the younger wife Saraswati angry and jealous and things came to a state when the disgusted Narahari stopped speaking to her. This made Saraswati even more angry and she decided to somehow get rid of Lakshmi and her son. With this in mind she began to look after Lakshmi and the child and Narahari again began talking to her. After some time he had to go abroad for his business and he prepared his fleet of ships. Then he bade farewell to his wives, telling them to take care of themselves and the child. His departure greatly distressed Lakshmi.

Now Saraswati began to plan the child's death while showering affection on him. Seeing this Lakshmi used to leave her son to Saraswati's care while she looked after the home. One day the son fell ill, arrangements were made for his treatment but the illness did not leave him. Saraswati nursed him all the time even forgetting to take her meals and this surprised the neighbours. In between her household duties Lakshmi used to inquire after the child, praying all the while to Goddess Prithvi (Earth) to cure him, promising to worship her till the last. Slowly the child got well and Lakshmi arranged the worship of Prithvi together with two other girls, while Saraswati began preparing the child's meal. Lakshmi painted Prithvi on the floor with rice paste and around this she painted the lotus flower and leaves. Then she poured honey, ghee (clarified butter) and milk into a conch shell and sat down to worship facing east.

Saraswati meanwhile was keeping watch. When she saw that Lakshmi had sat down to worship, she mixed poison with the food and gave it to the child. He cried out "mother" and then collapsed. Lakshmi appeared and saw the child had turned blue. She began crying beating her chest, others tried to console her and Saraswati got a trusted servant to throw the body in the river.

The body, however, did not drown, it floated along the river till a *sadhu* (holy man) saw it, picked it up and took it to his ashram. Then he plucked a leaf from a tree, squeezed it and as the juice was applied to the nose the child came back to life. The *sadhu* gave the boy warm milk to drink and kept him in the ashram.

Meanwhile Lakshmi continued to grieve her son's death, and Saraswati planned how to kill her also. One night as Lakshmi lay in her bed thinking of her husband and son, she saw her thatched roof had caught fire. She was mortally scared but could not get out. Outside Saraswati laughed like a she-devil and shouted, "I have killed the co-wife's son and now will kill her so that she cannot share my husband". At this stage a *sadhu* appeared, rescued Lakshmi and disappeared with her.

Saraswati then called out for the neighbours who came and doused the fire. They, however, found no trace of Lakshmi. Narahari also returned as he been worried over a bad dream. Seeing him Saraswati began wailing, "Didi (elder sister) died in a fire and the son died of illness. Suddenly the *sadhu* reappeared and said, You are not speaking the truth. It was you who killed them". With folded palms, Narahari asked, "Lord who are you"?

"I am the son of Prithvi who was pleased with your elder wife and on whose orders I have protected her and your son. Narahari said, "Lord please return to me my wife and son and I shall get rid of this unworthy woman right now". On hearing this Saraswati wept and said, "Kill me but do not leave me". The *sadhu* said, "What is this you are saying? You are a chaste woman and it is your duty to look after your husband. Get rid of your jealousy and anger, worship Prithvi with a pure mind and peace shall return to you".

Hearing these words Saraswati fell on the sadhu's feet. Lakshmi appeared with her son in her arms and the *sadhu* disappeared. From that day the two wives worshipped Prithvi, living in peace and harmony.

The elements of the fairy tale are clearly to be noticed in this brata tale. There is the jealousy of one wife towards another. The cruel acts she performs by feeding poison to the child and setting her co-wife's son fire, are common in fairy tales. The element of magic is provided by the bringing back to life of the dead child and the rescue of the wife from sure death.

Itu Brata

A highly popular brata. The story that is read out during the brata's observance also closely resembled a folk tale.

In a certain country lived a poor Brahmin, his wife and two daughters, Umno and Jhumno. They spent their days in great hardship.

One day the Brahmin felt like eating *pitha* (sweet pie) and said that to his wife.

The wife said, "where will I get rice, where will I get pulses, where will I get *gur* (molasses), oil and coconuts".

These words made the Brahmin sad. Every day he used to seek alms in six villages but that day he visited nine villages and collected all that was needed to make *pitha.* Returning home he told his wife, "now be careful don't give any to those useless daughters for if you do I will take them to the forest and leave them other. Now I am going for my bath and on return I shall eat the pithas".

The Brahmin, however, did not go for his bath. Instead he hid himself in a nearby corner with a rope in his hand.

The Brahmin waited. Every time his wife released a *pitha* in the frying pan it made a noise and he put a knot on the rope.

Meanwhile when a few *pithas* had been cooked, the elder daughter Umno came to the kitchen and said, "what is that you are frying mom, it smells nice please give me one".

The mother said, "Oh no, this is not for you, if the Brahmin finds out he will keep you in the forest".

Umno refused to listen. Weeping she pleaded for just one, saying, "please give me one, dad will never find out, I will not tell anybody".

Finding no way out, the mother gave her one and said, "eat it and go back to sleep just as you were sleeping earlier" Umno ate the *pitha* and then asked for another. Ultimately she had to be given half a *pitha* and her mother again told her to go back to sleep.

After Umno had gone came Jhumno. She was round five years old and the cleverer of the two. She also wanted a pitha.

The Brahmin's wife refused at first but then had to give her. Jhumno got one and liked it so much that she began asking for more. Ultimately she had to be given another half piece. Then she also was sent back to bed.

When the Brahmin heard no further noise of frying he realised that the cooking was over. Quickly he finished his bath in the pond, changed clothes and told his wife,

'I have the leaf here with me

Put *pitha* and rice on it'

The wife did as she was told. The Brahmin counted the knots on the rope and found that there were less *pithas* than knots. He became angry and wanted to know what happened to the others.

The wife said, "but I have given you the whole lot".

Brahmin said, "You have, have you? Then why are there three less? So you gave those to the girls. What I will send them to the forest". Then he finished eating, rinsed his mouth, woke up the girls and said, "Come I will take you to your aunt's place."

The girls were surprised as they had never heard they had an aunt but as their father said they did have one they followed him out of the house. Into the forest they went and walked a great distance when the children said they could walk no more. Their father said, "Okay let us take some rest. Here will I sit under the tree and you lie down resting your heads on my knees". The girls did so and soon were fast asleep.

Quietly the father got up and place two bricks under their heads. Then he spread round them some broken pieces of twigs, seeds of a fruit and a red paste which he had mixed with water. Having done this he went home.

It was nearly dark when the girls got up. All around they heard the roar of tigers and bears. Weeping, the elder Umno said, "Father has been eaten up by a tiger. Look his bones and blood are scattered all around". Jhumno said, however, "No father got angry because we ate the *pithas* and so he has left us in the forest. These are not bones and blood but broken reeds and red paste."

It was a huge banyan tree under which the girls were sitting. They put their sari ends round their necks and prayed to the tree to part its trunk so that they could find shelter inside it. The trunk opened and they got inside.

With morning the roar of wild animals died down and the girls again prayed to the tree, this time to ask for the trunk to part so that they could get out. The tree did that, they got out and began walking towards the rising sun in the east. After walking for quite some time they came across a large lake on the banks of which beautiful *gandharva* (demi gods) girls were making preparations for worship of some deity. As the two weeping children reached them they asked who they were and why were they weeping. Umno told them their story. The *gandharvas* took pity on them and asked them to worship Itu who will then surely help them.

The sisters asked, "But worship how? We know nothing".

The girls said, "That's no problem. Go to the lake, have your bath and we will allow you to share our worship".

The girls stepped inside the lake, and lo and behold, the water dried up. The dhobi who was doing his washing, the fishermen who was cleaning the fish he had caught, the women who were washing utensils, all stared in surprise and said, "What cursed girls. The water dried up as soon as they stepped in".

The sisters again broke out in tears and returned to the *gandharvas* to say what had happened. They, however, said there was nothing to worry, made a ring out of *kush* (a kind of holy grass) and told the sisters, "Now go and drop this in the lake and the water will reappear". They did so, water again filled the lake, people resumed their work and the sisters had their bath.

The *gandharvas* helped the girls to worship the deity and said, "Now seek what you want from the deity". The girls wanted to know what they should seek and the *gandharvas* said, "Say that you want your father to remember you". The girls did that.

The next Sunday again the sisters worshipped Itu with the *gandharvas*. This time Umno sought a king as her husband and Jhumno a minister's son.

The Sunday after they requested the deity to give their father a son as he had none.

Came another Sunday and the sisters desired that their father who was illiterate be made the king's court pundit. On the last day of the month of Poush they prayed that their father who was poor be made rich.

A few days passed when the Brahmin suddenly thought of his daughters. He went to the forest and as he began calling out for them, they appeared. He hugged them and brought them back home.

Some time later the king's father died and the king made a public announcement that he who was really a pundit should hold a gold basket which was displayed. The sisters caught the basket as the announcer was passing by their hut and took it to their father.

The Brahmin was aghast. "What have you done?", he asked. "Only a great pundit is allowed to hold this and I know nothing". The girls assured him there was nothing to be scared of, he should go to the king's court where he would be made the court pundit.

"How will that happen?", asked the father.

"As soon as you utter the Sanskrit letter K will roll out of your mouth", said the girls.

In the king's court the Brahmin found others debating various issues related to the scriptures in Sanskrit. He stood listening and suddenly he uttered 'K' and as soon as he did that Sanskrit slokas began to come out of his mouth. This pleased the king and her made him the court pundit. He also made him the teacher of his son and that of the minister.

In one year the two became great scholars and to please their teacher they wanted to marry his two two daughters.

A highly pleased Brahmin began making arrangements for the marriage. Umno was then nine and Jhumno seven.

After the marriage when the time came for the daughters to leave with their husbands and Umno was about to climb on an elephant's back with the price, Jhumno said, "Sister you have forgotten the earthen pitcher of Itu". Umno replied, "Now I am married to a price why should I bother about an earthen pot". Jhumno reminded her that they owed their good fortune to Itu but she paid no heed to these words, got on the elephant and went away.

Jhumno did not neglect her pitcher. With it she climbed on to another elephant with the minister's son and they also went but along a different path.

Disaster struck along the path that Umno had taken. Cattle died, houses collapsed, people died, everywhere there was the sound of wailing.

Jhumno saw only prosperity around her. Houses were being built, ponds were being dug, marriages were taking place, trees were in full bloom. She saw only happiness around her.

When Umno reached the palace, the king's mother came to welcome her with a gold winnow. But as soon as she touched Umno's forehead with it, the winnow became one of cane. The king's mother shivered in fright.

At the minister's house the newly wed wife was greeted with a cane winnow which turned into gold as did utensils made of brass. Everybody cheered, the bride had brought luck to the family.

Meanwhile the Brahmin became wealthy, a son was born to him and his wife never forgot to worship Itu as had been advised by Jhumno. The son grew up and in time became a learned person. Then the time came for his marriage.

It was a Sunday in the month of Aghrayan when the son went to get married accompanied by others inlcuding the barber who had to be present on such occasions. Midway it was realised that the customary nut cracker had been left behind and the Brahmin ran back home. He began calling his wife but could not see her. Then he discovered that she had sat down to worship Itu.

This angered the Brahmin. How could his wife think that her worship of the deity was more important than attending to him. His newly acquired wealth had made him very proud and so he kicked away the water filled pitcher which had been kept for Itu's worship:

Itu went rolling,
Filaria struck the leg.

In no time the Brahmin's property vanished, his son died on the way and he became so stricken by filaria that he found it difficult to move around.

Things were no better at Umno's kingdom. At the palace elephants did and so did horses. Then one day the king died.

The last rites of the king were to be performed and Umno had go the river for her bath. The road was cleared. However, there was a piece of glass on which she stepped and cut her foot.

Weeping, Umno returned to the palace and complained to the prince against the sweeper who had neglected to sweep away the glass. This so angered the prince that he went to the sweeper's house and cut his head off. Then he was filled with remorse as he thought he had been a little too hasty.

Returning to the palace the prince, actually now the king, told Umno, "I need to cheer myself up. Come let us play dice".

The dice board was brought and they began playing. After sometimes Queen Umno felt sleepy and yawned. Immediately the king's moustache was singed.

The king got scared. What an unlucky queen is this whose yawn singed my moustache, he told himself. He ordered her out of the kingdom. Umno went to the kingdom of Jhumno, crying all the way.

She, however, did not dare enter through the main gate and so stood near the door at the back. There she saw maids carrying water in gold pitchers. Umno asked for whom were they taking the water and they replied, "For our Queen Jhumno so that she can have her bath". Umno told them to tell the queen that a sister of her had come and wanted to see her.

When the maids returned for more water, Umno asked them whether they had informed the queen. They said they had forgotten and asked to be given something which will remind them of her request. Umno took a creeper, shaped it like a ring and dropped it into the water.

The maids took the water inside and when the queen poured it on herself the creeper fell on her and she wanted to know what it was. The maids said, "Oh yes, we forgot. Some one who says she is a sister of yours is waiting by the rear door".

Jhumno remembered how her sister had neglected the pitcher when going off with her housband and how she had feared that this would bring bad luck to her. She told the maids to bring her sister in. When they did that she ordered them to bathe Umno well with oil and water. When they did that she dressed Umno in proper clothes and said, "Sister this is why I had asked you to take Itu's pitcher with you, for we owe very thing to Itu".

Umno began living with Jhumno. Came the month of Aghrayan and Jhumno said, "We have to worship Itu". Then when Sunday came, Jhumno completed all arrangements and asked her main to bring her sister.

Umno came and said, "Sorry, I cannot join in the worship for when I was feeding your sons a grain of puffed rice fell on the ground and I picked it up and ate it. This distressed Jhumno who told herself that there was more hardship in store for Umno.

Came another Sunday and Jhumno again reminded her sister of the Itu worship. But again she could not participate as this time she had licked from the ground a bit of jaggery, Jhumno was displeased but did not say anything.

When the next Sunday came, Jhumno tied the end of her sari with that of Umno. Then she took her for the ritual bath, completed all arrangements and together they worshipped the deity. When the time came to ask for a boon, Jhumno said, "Sister ask that the king's wealth be returned to her". Umno did as she was told to do.

The king got back his wealth, grew a new moustache and began to pine for Umno. He sent out his men to find her but nowhere could they find her. The king was sorely disappointed and one day asked the minister, "Has she by any chance gone to your place".

The minister gave no reply but on his advice Jhumno one day invited the king. After he finished his meal, a smiling Jhumno brought her sister to him and said, "Here she is Your Majesty, but you cannot take her with you. Just as you had harassed her so must you decorate the entire road from here to your palace. Just as my sister came alone so she will return alone",

Gladly the king did as he was asked to do. Umno returned carrying the pitcher of water this time. On her way she saw the body of the sweeper and the head which had been severed by the king. The sight filled her with great sorrow. Talking the name of Itu she sprinkled some water from the pitcher on the body and the head, the two became one and the sweeper became alive. All those who saw this were filled with wonder. The maids who were accompanying Umno called out, "Long live devi Itu".

Jhumno's parents were finding it very difficult to make both ends meet. On many days they had to go without food. One day, her mother told her father, "Go to Jhumno and see what you can get".

Angrily the Brahmin replied, "As if she will flood us with money and things. Do children do that"?

The wife, however, was insistent. "When she hears of our condition she will certainly give something". Then she begged for a piece of soap, got it, washed the Brahmin's tattered clothes and sent him to Jhumno's house.

The Brahmin reached Jhumno's house. Seeing his condition, Jhumno wept and at the same time realised that the curse of Itu had fallen on them as her mother no longer worshipped her.

Jhumno fed her father and packed some money, clothes and food into a bundle and said, "Father I am giving you a man who will carry this bundle home".

The Brahmin said, "No need, I will be able to carry it myself".

Jhumno assured him that the man won't have to be paid, that he will just reach the bundle home and come back.

The Brahmin said nothing more and set out for home with the man carrying the bundle. After they had gone some distance the thought that he would have to give something to the man from what he was carrying again disturbed him. He took the bundle from the man and sent him away. Then he resumed his journey with the bundle on his head.

A little later the Brahmin reached a pond. He was thirsty and thought he would have a drink. Hiding the bundle behind a tree, he washed his feed, drank and then began looking for his bundle. But it was gone. Then he said to himself, "This must be the work of that daughter of mine. She had given those things just to show off and at the same time had made arrangements for snatching the bundle away". Then he returned home.

The bundle meanwhile had flown away and entered Jhumno's storeroom. When Jhumno saw it she opened it and found it contained all that she had given her father. She said, "Father is going through a bad spell. One cannot enjoy what he gets unless the time comes for that".

At her parents' house her mother was clearly disappointed to see her husband return empty handed. "Jhumno gave you nothing", she asked.

The Brahmin said, "I told you all these people are the same".

The wife again asked, "Did she give you nothing"?

The Brahmin said, "Oh yes, she did pack a big bundle and had also given a servant to carry it so that he could run away with it which he did when I went to the pond for a wash and a drink".

The wife said nothing more. After a couple of days the Brahmin told her, "Why don't you go to Jhumno's house and eat well for a few days". That was exactly what the wife was wanting to do. She got into a litter and went to her daughter's house.

When they reached the door, the litter gave away and she fell down, badly hurting herself. The litter bearers said,

Comes minister's mom-in-law

Falls and breaks her skull

Put down litter, put down

On hearing this servants and maids rushed out and carried her inside.

Seeing her mother, Jhumno cried and said, "Mother why are you all suffering so much"?

The mother told her how the Brahmin had kicked away Itu's pitcher.

Jhumno took good care of her mother. Then when the month of Aghrayan came she worshipped Itu with her mother and asked her to seek the deity's blessings.

Respectfully the mother prayed for her husband's reinstatement as the court pundit.

On the next three Sundays she prayed for the return of her husband's wealth, the birth of any her son and lastly for good sense to always prevail on him.

All her prayers were answered, they got back everything and the Brahmin came to take his wife back home. Jhumno told her father, "Never forget that we would not have got anything if Itu had not blessed us".

Days passed by and then the chariot came from heaven to take away Queen Jhumno. All began to weep but she told them to be ever faithful to Itu and worship her for peace and prosperity. Then she dressed herself and smiling all the while got into the chariot which rose towards the sky from where the gods showered flower petals on her.

All the elements of a folk tale are present in this story.

Sending children away to the forest is common in folk tales.

The element of magic is provided by the tree parting its trunk. Also by the dead sweeper returning to life after Umno sprinkled Itu's water on his body and severed head.

The role played by fate is seen in the marriages of Umno and Jhumno to the prince and the minister's son.

The brata essentially is a part of worship of the tree which is a symbol of Karam, the deity Karam. With the worship has blended belief in the powers of magic. The deity is worshipped by Hindus and tribals alike for better crops and thereby prosperity. In this tale the features of a folk tale are clearly noticed. There is the merchant who had everything, home, cattle, crops and two sons both of whom had become rich, Dharam by trading and Karam through agriculture. But they ran out of luck and were forced to become labourers.

If the brothers had lost everything because of their own fault, the element of chance and availing it is introduced by the way in which Karam could please the king and regain his fortune.

The third element of a folktale, surprise, is brought into the *brata katha* by the talking animals and trees and women with various things that stuck to their bodies. Finally it is the power of magic that resolves all problems.

Then there is the *Prithvi* (earth) *Brata* which is observed to bring rain and was born out of the primitive man's belief that this could be done through a magic ritual.

The story is about a trader, Narahari and his two wives Lakshmi and Saraswati. A son was born to the first and so she became Narahari's favourite which caused Saraswati to become jealous and to decide that she would do away with both Lakshmi and her son. Once when Narahari was away from home on business the son fell ill but recovered after Lakshmi is entreaties to the deity Prithvi. He, however, died when Saraswati mixed poison in his food. His heart-broken mother immersed the body in the river but instead of drowning it floated some distance and was discovered by a hermit who brought the body back to life and kept him in the hermitage.

Meanwhile Saraswati decided to do away with Lakshmi also and set her one night set her room on fire. As the flames shot up a hermit arrived and took Lakshmi away. Narahari returned and was told that his first wife and son had died. At this stage the hermit arrived again and said that Saraswati was not speaking the truth. He revealed himself as the son of Prithvi, got Lakshmi and her son back and advised Saraswati to worship Prithvi to cleanse her mind of jealousy.

Various elements noticed in a folklore are present here, such as jealousy, cruelty, magic (the revival of the boy and the rescue of the mother from certain death).

Jampukur Brata's Alpana.

7

Brata : Bengali Poetry in the Old and Middle Ages

The *brata* being an integral part of a woman's life in rural Bengal, it was only natural that it should find its place in literature over the ages, particularly in the various *Mangal Kavyas*, devoted to the deities. In other writings also there are many references to the rules of the *brata*, the consequences of these not being observed properly, forcible observance of the *brata* by kings and landlords etc.

Some examples are given below:

Kashiram Das says in the *Shanti Parva* of Mahabharata:

"She who observes a *brata* with a clean mind
Cleans herself of her sins".

Maladhar Bose says in *Sri Krishna Vijaya.*

"Bathe naked in the Yamuna
Yours *brata* will go waste."

Manasa Brata: Manasa is the deity of snakes and she must be appeased. Also if she is pleased then a woman will rid herself of her barrenness, blindness and leprosy are cured, lost things are recovered and the dead return to life. In *Manasa Mangal* (the poem for the *brata*) a detailed account is given of when the deity should be worshipped and how a tree is worshipped as her symbol.

In *Purba Banga Gitika* we find,

"Why the sound of drum beat,
It's the king worshipping Manasa
On the last day of Sravana".

The *Gitika* also contains woman's prayers to Manasa so that their husbands may come home.

In Mymensingh Gitika edited by Dinesh Chandra Sen we find:

(a) Sāyan masete loke puje manasā

In the month of Sravan do people worship Manasa

(b) Kiser dhāk kiser dhol kiser vādya bāje
Śāyana sankrānte rājā manasāre puje

Why the sound of drums and other instruments

On the last day of Sravan the king worships Manasa

(c) Śāyan bāona mās ākhāl bākhāl pāni
Manasā pujite kanya haila utjogini

Month of Sravan, water all round

Girl got ready to worship Manasa

Then the rhyme goes on to describe the preparations made and ends with

Śeer noāiya kare śatek pannati

"Bar dāo manasā go ghare āyok pati"

Bends her head and offers hundred prayers

"Bless me manasa let husband come home"

The *Dashara* and *Arfa bratas* are other variations of the *Manasa Brata* in that the same deity is worshipped for the fulfillment of wishes, Mention is found in *Manasa Vijaya* and *Manasa Purana.*

Dashara brata: It is another version of Manasa *brata* and the purpose is again to clear the mind of fear of snakes. It is also associated with the *Panchami brata* and some communities plant the manasa branch on the day of Dusshera and worship it on the day of Panchami. In *Manasa Puran* (edited by Asutosh Das, 1980) it is said,

"On the day of Dusshera in the month of Jaistha
Shall people worship Manasa Panchami".

(Dusahara is the tenth day of the lunar fortnight in the month of Jaistha and Panchami the fifth lunar day of either fornight.)

Arfa brata: Another worship of Manasa in the month of Bhadra. On the previous night rice and vegetables are cooked and offered to the deity and eaten the next day by all. In *Manasa Mangal* Ketakadas Khemananda has said,

People shall worship you in the month of Bhadra.

This (the worship) shall be known as Arfa *brata* in the world".

Chandi Brata: Observed on Tuesday for general well being and so it is also known as Mangal Chandi. Speaking of the purpose of the *brata* Mukundaram Chakravarti said in his *Chandi Mangal Kavya*:

"Arrived Chandika in the Kali yuga
To fulfill wishes of all.

Brahmin shall turn to religion listening to this
Kshatriya will gain success in battle.
Vaisya on listening will turn to commerce
Sudra shall gain pleasure of emancipation".

Mukundaram also instructs:

Worship Chandika every Tuesday
Durga shall steer you through the sea of troubles.

Sasthi Brata: Observed for the well being of children. The *brata* is also observed every month of the year and is then known as *Baro Sasthi*, '*baro*' meaning twelve. Krishnaram Das says in *Sasthi Mangal*:

"Woman who worships Sasthi twelve times a year
Disease and sorrow she need not fear".

One of the many forms of Sasthi worship is the Jamai Sasthi when the 'jamai' or son-in-law is feted and his well-being desired along with that of other children. The *brati* should not eat fish or meat and Krishnaram Das says, "awful is the sight of a woman eating non-vegetarian food on Jamai Sasthi day".

The *Sasthi Mangal* is treated as a *brata katha* from the earliest days with some variations in West Bengal and Bangladesh. In the West Bengal version a young woman gets back her six children with the grace of Sasthi after losing them because of her greed for good food. In the Bangladesh version she brings all kinds of disasters to her family after stealing the food offered to the deity and ultimately gets rid of the curse by satisfying Yama.

Certain rules have to be strictly followed. If the sixth day (Sasthi) of the fortnight falls on a Monday or a Saturday then the *brata* is not observed as it is believed that the *brati* will suffer. So Krishnaram Das says:

"If Sasthi falls on a Monday
The worship will only be in heaven.
No worship shall take place on earth
If a woman does so childless she shall be.
If Sasthi falls on a Saturday
Worship shall take place only in the nether world.
On Sunday, Friday, Wednesday and Thursday
Worship all women with children."

In his *Dharma Mangal* Manikram Ganguly has spoken of the customs associated with the observance of the *brata.* The ingredients he speaks of are, Ganga water, bananas, sandal paste and sweets.

Surya Brata: Worship of the Sun in the hope of being as powerful as him and performed by both men and women. Mention of the *brata* is found in different literary works as in the Mahabharat of Kashiram Das:

"Suffer pains and observe the *brata* of Sun worship".
In the *Padma Purana* of Vijaygupta is said,
"Who observes Surya *brata* on Sundays
Enters the gates of Sun in his Sun chariot".

Ekadasi Brata: Observed by widows only by fasting. The *Padma Purana* says,

She who eats only once on the *brata* day
Will enter the gates of Vishnu's world in His chariot".

Lakshmi Brata: Deity of wealth and prosperity, Lakshmi has to be worshipped on Thursday in the months of *Bhadra, Poush* and *Chaitra* if the desired result is to be achieved. It is said in the Mahabharata that the gods had rescued Lakshmi after churning the sea. Pranab Kumar Sinha says, according to the Bengali proverb Lakshmi's blessings are earned through business and in the olden days Bengali traders had become wealthy by trading across the seas (*or churning the seas-translator*). In East Bengal, Lakshmi's carrier was not the owl but the boat. Thus, the ritual of worshipping Lakshmi is essentially one of the trading community.

Most Bengali homes, however, observe the ritual on Thursdays when the alpana is painted on the floor of the room, *Purba Banga Gitika* gives a vivid account of how this is painted. On preparing the rice-paste, a woman first draws the feet of her parents, then sheaves of corn, Siva and Durga and Lakshmi on lotus leaf.

Ananta Brata: Observed by married women. The Mahabharata of Kashiram Das says the day of the ritual used to be announced in the town with the playing of musical instruments.

Dharma Brata: Mentioned in the *Dharma Mangal Kavya*, the ritual can be observed by all for getting cured of ailments or for getting children. Women considered it a sin to leave the observance of a ritual half way through and the Mahabharata says:

> "Not right for a chaste woman to stop a ritual mid-way". The epic tells the story of Raja Chandraketu who had died because he did not complete a ritual and was reborn only after doing so in the next world.

The literature of the old and middle ages often speak of kings and landlord forcing their subjects to observe certain rituals with the warning,

> "who does not observe the *ekadasi* (fasting) *brata* will have to leave the country for sure".

The Mahabharata tells of how people of all castes observed the *Ananta Brata* for fear of incurring the king's wrath if they did not do so.

Satyapir Brata: The story of Satyapir brings to us a picture of harmony among the ancient mythologies (Puranas) of both the Hindus and Muslims. The narrative speaks of a poor Brahmin becoming rich by pleasing a Muslim saint. Taheer Mahmud's *Brata Katha* of Satyapir tells the story of the birth of Satyapir as an illegitimate child of Sandhyabati, daughter of the demon *Moy.* He was born with supernatural powers (like the child Krishna) and 'punished' the demon. (*Muhammad Abu Taleb, Eighteenth Century Poets, Journal of the Bangla Academy*). The ritual is essentially about appeasing a *Pir* or a Muslim saint for getting the object that is desired.

There are many references to the observance of the *brata* and the rules in *Mymensingh Gitika* and *Purba Banga Gitika.* In the latter there is the tale of Bagula who spurns the overtures of the prince to marry the merchant's son. Instead of getting into a conflict with the prince she pretends she is in the midst of observing a ritual and requests him not to make her end it midway. Bhelua in *Bhelua Sundari* play had also resorted to similar ruse. So the *brata* was useful in other ways also in those ancient times.

Rane Eo Brata's Alpana

8

Brata : Sociological Analysis

One of the striking features of the observance of these rituals or *bratas*, is the role of women. At a time when society was seen as being dominated by men, the women of the family had actually occupied an important position. Dilip Kumar Lahiri and Bhaswati Lahiri have said:

> "When a male dominated Brahminical society had laid the responsibility of praying for their welfare on the shoulders of men priests, in Bengal it was the women who took up the task to be performed by the classless women priests or 'bratis'. It has to be noticed that unlike the male priests, these women did not necessarily have to be Brahmins and were truly 'secular'. They prayed for the general good, keeping their personal interests away which could not have been said of the male priests. The male dominated society, however, has never sought to evaluate the role that these 'brati's played in the task of social reforms". (*Lokasanskriti Patrika*).

The *Brata Katha* is a part of folklore. The tales or katha's are not mere expression of wishes but also carry the story of a hard reality in which struggle was a part of life. The tales symbolise the daily struggle against repression by a people ridden with poverty. It will perhaps be useful to take a look at some of the *bratas* from the sociological point of view:

Punyipukur Brata: During the hot summer months water would be (as even now it is) scarce in the villages and it was the women who had to make arrangements for it. The ritual marked a belief in divine help. The narrative of the *brata* speaks of a poor Brahmin family which had to leave home as the landlord's rent could not be paid, because of repeated crop failures. It was midday when they reached a pond where the daughter observed her *Punyipukur Brata* and God arrived in the shape of an old man and asked for food. The family had no surplus food to give him so the daughter gave her share to the man who ate it, was satisfied and disappeared. As the surprised family looked around, they heard a voice in the sky blessing the girl with good fortune. The next day the king came and said he had a dream in which he had been ordered to get his son married to the daughter.

Like all such narrations the story speaks of a man's helplessness in the face of a cruel nature and equally cruel social superiors.

Savitri Brata: Observed by married women, sometimes for fourteen years at a stretch. While observing it, the woman must eat only once a day but nothing that has been cultivated with the plough. It is aimed at ensuring a long life for the husband and also his welfare. Inherent is the ancient belief in magic and also the essential features of a patriarchal society in which all prayers were directed towards the man's welfare and also for male children. The related narration also reflects an acceptance of man's superiority over women as the ritual ends with the 'brati' washing the feet of the husband and offering him fruits and one hundred and eight grains of rice.

Maghmandal Brata: Sun worship. The ritual is observed during the whole of the winter month of Magh (mid January to mid February) for five years. The chant of the ritual describes the marriage of Sun.

The form of the ritual captures the ancient practice of worshipping Sun, trees, the earth and crops. The ritual is observed by girls from the age of five which means that even in that early age they are taught that they have nothing to look forward to personally; the prayers are all for the male members of the family. This was perhaps a natural outcome of the transition from hunting to cultivating when gradually men began playing a more dominant role.

The chant of the ritual also brings this out. The girls pray that with the blessings of Sun, they would become daughters of rich men and daughters-in-law of the wealthy. Never is it said that directly they would acquire wealth as it was not possible in that society.

Raeed Raja's Kichha (tale): This *Brata Katha* is to be found in the Bengali dominated Barak Valley of Assam. The ritual is observed on Thursdays by unmarried girls or married women, It is observed to save crops from excessive rain and those observing it must not touch any non-vegetarian food.

The story is about two countries, one of clouds where Meghraja rules (Megh-Cloud) and the other of sunshine ruled by Raeed Raja (Raeed—sunlight). In the land of clouds the people can eat only fruits and aquatic plants, while in the latter they have no problem as plenty of paddy is grown.

The princess of the land of sunshine gets to marry the prince of the land of clouds and when leaving for her husband's home takes with her a bit of sunshine and some paddy. In her husband's country she found the food inedible and so got out a little sunlight, dried a bit of paddy and cooked rice. Nobody, however, wanted to eat that strange food and ultimately, persuaded by her entreaties, the king ordered his minister to eat it. Trembling, he did so, fell asleep and on waking up said he must have rice every day.

Now with the year gone, the princess had to cook rice each day with her sunlight and paddy which she did in a locked room. One day the queen, curious about what was going on, opened the door, the sunlight escaped and filled the country. At first the people were scared but were assured by the princess that nothing was wrong. Then when the time came for her to visit her own country, she took a bit of cloud with her and in this way the two countries got what they lacked.

The story not only speaks of wish fulfillment but also fear of the unknown and the absolute authority of feudal lords before which everybody had to bow down, like the reluctant minister eating the rice. Also the people in the land of clouds symbolise the inequal distribution of wealth even in those ancient times, they not being blessed with that which their neighbours had.

Women, we have seen, played a key role in the observance of the *brata*. These allowed them temporary escape from the routine of daily chores inside the house. The very nature of the rituals allowed women to sing, recite, dance, paint and listen to stories without anybody looking down upon them because of the religious connotation. At the same time their inherent sense of discipline becomes obvious from the strict adherence to the laid down code of conduct for each ritual. What should also be noticed is that while men were the dominant players in life in general, inside the house, in the bosom of the family, it was the women who ruled, not only taking care of everybody but also praying for their welfare. The mother of course has always occupied the highest place in the Indian family system.

The *brata* is essentially a worship of the powers of magic and production and is an essential part of life in an agrarian society. Having grown out of ancient practices, these rituals reflect the cultural mix that took place with the arrival of the Aryans. In his sociological study of Bengal's folk culture, Benoy Ghosh has noticed that these rituals of women took shape at a time when self interest in a class divided society took precedence over social interest. The *brata* in its true spirit is, however, pre-class or classless.

Regarding the belief in the magical powers of the *brata* James George Frazer has said (*The Golden Bough : A Study in Magic and Religion*) that it has been seen that such rituals have brought the rains down or stopped them. Similarly Benoy Ghosh sees nothing wrong on the part of the ancient man to believe in the powers of the ritual just because they fail at times. It may be just a coincidence that a ritual brings down the rain but what of that? The forecasts of the meteorologists do not always come true but that does not prevent them from making daily forecasts.

Even with modernisation, the rituals have not died down in the villages. The change that time has brought is external, deep inside the faith in the rituals continues to flow. Like Iswari Patuni in Bharatchandra Roy's *Annada Mangal*, inside every woman's heart lives the prayer, "Let my son live amidst plenty". The nature of the desires having remained essentially the same, how can faith, in the means of fulfilling these, disappear?

9

Various Bratas

Starting with the last day of the Bengali month of *Chaitra* (mid April), the *bratas* are observed throughout the year. There is never any pomp associated with these, the *bratas*, being essentially domestic rituals performed by women for various purposes. Now let us take a look at some of these:

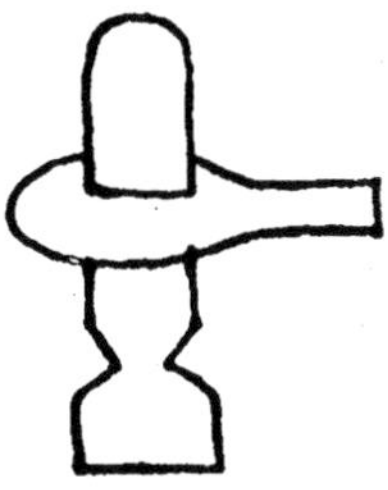

Siva Brata.

Siva Brata: Observed throughout *Vaisakh,* the first month in the Bengali calendar, by girls and unmarried women in the hope of getting husbands like *Siva.* The ritual has to be observed for at least four consecutive years for the wish to be fulfilled. The essential ingredients are, earth from the banks of the Ganga, *Akanda* (sunplant) flower. *dhutura* (datura) flower, leaves of the *bel* (wood-apple) tree, grass, rice, white sandalwood, bananas etc. Small idols of Siva are made of clay, bathed and offered fruits, the girls and women chanting all the while. Married women also perform the ritual for the welfare of their children.

Dasputtal Brata: Observed by unmarried girls throughout the month of *Vaisakh* and for five years. Ten dolls are made of rice-paste and while worshipping these with white sandalwood, *tulsi* (basil) leaves etc, they voice their desires for husbands like Rama, father-in-law like Dasarath, mother-in-law like Kaushalya, to have sons like Kunti and be a cook like Draupadi.

Gokal Brata: Observed for the welfare of cattle from the last day of the month of *Chaitra.* Girls can participate once they are five years old. The horns of the cow are washed and smeared with oil, paste of turmeric, sandalwood and vermillion is applied on the forehead and some grass and banana is given as feed. "With this feed to the cow, may I go to heaven", goes the chant. They also pray for the destruction of all insects, flies and mosquitoes (in the interest of the cow's comfort) and for gold bangles and lives without co-wives for themselves.

Eo Sankranti Brata: A married woman is known as *eo* and the ritual is for staying such. The 'bratini' washes the feet of other married women, puts the vermillion mark of (indicating married status) on their foreheads, combs their hair and presents them with bangles of conchshell and iron which are also indicative of the same status.

A similar *brata* is the *Nitya Sindoor Brata.* Nitya Sindoor means daily application of the vermillion mark.

There are a number of other *bratas* observed by married women for avoiding widowhood and retaining the love of their husbands. These are the *Rupa Haldi, Ada Haldi, Tejodarpan, Chhatusankranti,* etc. The observance of all these begin on the last day of *Chaitra* and involving feting other married women and sometimes Brahmins. In the last named *brata* barley or maize flour is offered to a married women along with molasses. The flour is known as *chhatu.*

Prithvi (earth) Brata: observed by unmarried girls. Alpana designs of lotus leaves are painted as also of the earth deity and the offerings include clarified butter, milk, honey. The deity is urged to take the sweets and make the girls wives of kings.

Punyipukur Brata.

Punyipukur Brata: For water during the dry season. A hole is dug in the courtyard (symbol of pond or *pukur*) which is filled with water and branches of the *bel* tree and basil are planted in the hole. The prayer is for the family's welfare which will not be possible unless the rains come and wet the fields.

Asvathapata Brata.

Asvathapata (leaves of the peepul tree) Brata: Essentially tree worship, its purpose is to avoid widowhood, get good children, wealth and peace. The women performing the ritual have to carry five leaves of the tree on their heads and dip in the pond five times. Each leaf is a prayer for remaining married till old age, golden complexion, son, prosperity and peace. In some places it is known as the *Asvathanarayan Brata.*

Harir Charan Brata.

Harir Charan Brata: Observed during the month of Vaisakh by both married and unmarried women. Two feet of the Lord (Harir Charan) are painted with white sandalwood paste on a copper vessel and the prayer is for a happy family. The one whose wishes are granted,

"See not the death of husband or son
Nor the deaths of friends her own".

Tulsi Brata: Observed on the first day of *Vaisakh.* Needed are a basil tree and a clay pot with holes. After her bath an elderly or married women pours water on the pot so that it seeps through the holes and drops on the tree. The chant runs:

'Tulsi, Tulsi, Brindaban
Tulsi, you are God
As I pour water on your head
So will I enjoy the benefits (of your blessings)'.

Basudhara Brata.

Basudhara Brata: Another ritual to appease the rain God, during summer.

Mangal Chandi Brata: Observed for the happiness and welfare of children and performed on Tuesdays which in Bengali is called *Mangal* meaning the same as the ritual's objective. The ritual can be observed throughout the year, the ingredients being jackfruits leaves, bel (wood-apple) leaves and basil, 17 grains of paddy, 17 grains of maize and fruits. The paddy and maize are husked and then the rice, maize, basil and one banana are mixed in a mound and divided into three portions. Each portion has to be swallowed in three mouthfuls, taking care that nothing touches the teech. Three sips of water follow and the rest of the ingredients is thrown into a pond.

Bipattarini Brata: To be protected against all kinds of *bipad* or danger. Observed in the first Tuesday or Saturday, whichever comes first, after the *Ratha Yatra* or Chariot Festival in the month of Asadh, the third in the Bengali calendar. Thirteen flowers, fruits, pies made from rice, 13 strands of red thread, betel-leaves, betel nuts, flour, etc., are needed for the ritual.

Janmashtami brata: To celebrate the birth of Krishna, the Saviour of all. Observed in the month of *Sravana,* the fourth in the Bengali calendar in the midst of the rainy season.

Sivamusti Brata: To worship *Shiva* with half a fistful of paddy, rice, wheat and pulses. Beginning on a Monday in the month of *Sravana,* it is observed for five years, to bring good fortune to husbands.

Bhaduli Brata: Observed in the month of *Bhadra,* fifth in the Bengali calendar, it is to wish a safe return for those who had left home on work. The prayer was meant essentially for traders who returned home after the rainy season either by the land or water route. One of the chants of the *brata* says:

'River, river where do you go
Bring news as you flow.
News of my brother, husband and father-in-law
River, river tell me of them as you flow'.

Kukkuti Brata: The *kukkuti* or her is considered a symbol of fertility and its worship, it is believed, brings many children. Bengali women have adopted this from the tribals, particularly the Oraons.

Garsi Brata: Observed in the last day of *Asvin* and before sunrise. Small idols or rice-paste are made to represent the three deities, Lakshmi, Kumber and Narayan and jute stalks are lit. In this ritual boys are not supposed to share the offerings made to the deities as it is believed that would make them insensitive. The *brata* is for the family's welfare.

Veerashtami Brata: Observed to make sons courageous on the eighth (*ashtami*) day of the Durga Puja festival.

Kojagari Lakshmi Brata: A major *brata* of women, this is observed on the full moon night of the month of *Ashvin* to worship Lakshmi, the goddess of wealth. The alpana is painted, the principal motif being footmarks and sheaves of corn. Abanindranath Tagore has spoken of a similar festival in far away Peru where the idol of the deity is made of maize.

Kojagari Lakshmi Brata.

There is also the *Alakshmi Brata* observed on the dark might of Kali Puja in the month of *Kartick*. An idol is made of cowdung with the left hand and placed in the open on a wooden seat. The priest does not look at it and only throws a few flowers at it with his left hand. After this the idol is kept covered, taken away from the house, the cover is removed and it is destroyed with a chopper.

The Alakshmi is the deity of crops and in ancient times used to be worshipped as Lakshmi. Abanindranath Tagore has referred to the worship of the same deity in Mexico where the women let their hair flow down and pray that their crops be as long as their hair. (*Banglar Brata: Abanindranath Tagore*).

Bhootchaturdasi Brata: Once observed in many Bengali homes on the night before the worship of Kali to free homes of the influence of *bhoots* (ghosts) and evil spirits. Not much in practice these days.

Itu Brata: Observed to get good husbands, children and wealth. The chant says, she who observes this *brata* gets rid of the stigma of barrenness. The fertility theme also has *Itu* as a provider of crops.

Senjuti Brata: Observed throughout the month of *Aghrayan.* The alpana is a must and 52 motifs are painted. Each picture is a symbol of the various emotions of woman and each is worshipped with the singing of the relevant chant. For instance the chant for the 'palki' (palanquin) motif is, "I travel by *dola* (palki) and see my face in a mirror of gold", the palan duin being a symbol of prosperity. For the painting of moon and sun, the women sing that as they worship the moon and sun so may they have gold and silver. There are prayers for as many brothers as there are stars. One of the pictures is that of a bed and the accompanying chant speaks of a comfortable and happy life. While painting the pictures of ornaments with rice-paste, the women sing, "May my own ornaments be of gold".

The chants of the *brata* repeatedly make clear the women's dislike for co-wives. One of the paintings is of crow and the bird is asked to take away such a wife and drown her in the river and the prayer for the *hata* (ladle) is, "*hata, hata, hata, khā satiner mathā*"—ladle, ladle, ladle eat my co-wife's head. Barrenness for her is also desired and even death.

The women also pray for the prosperity of the whole family. So while painting a cowshed, they sing for a real one of their own. Prayers are sung not only for the parents but also the in-laws.

Senjuti Brata-Motifs and Prayers

Motifs and accompanying rhymes of the *Senjuti Brata*:

1. Evening prayer Senjuti
   16 *bratis* in 16 squares
   I sit in one
   Pray for wealth and sons
   Fill parents' home

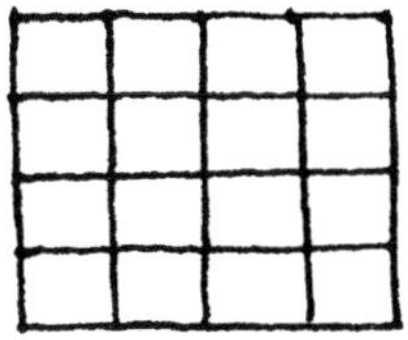

2. O Lord Shankar, save me
   (from being) a fool's wife

3. Elephants and horses,
   Servants and the Queen
   Sitting back against bolsters
   Happy with love of all.

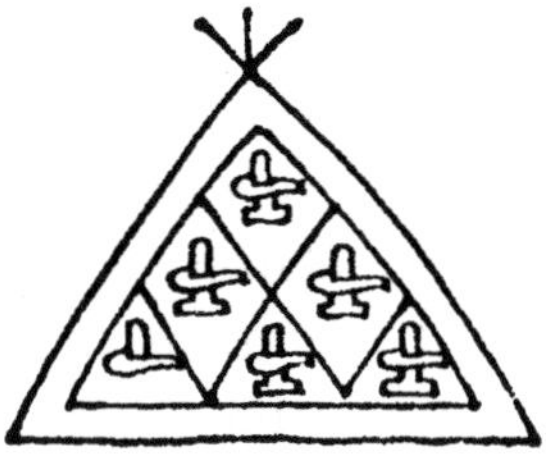

4. Come by *dola* (palanuin),
return by *dola*
See face in gold mirror,
Ghee and madhu they both eat
Travel as they do.

5. Worship Ganga Yamuna
Eat from gold plates.

6. Worship Sun and Moon
Sweets from a gold bowl
Gold to wear for me.

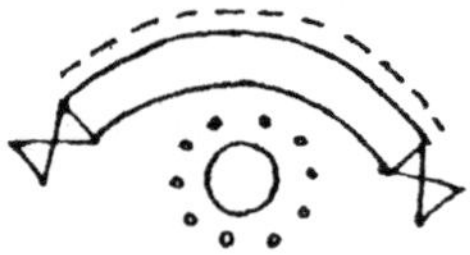

7. May I have as many brothers
As there are the stars
Who I worship.

8. Floods are coming
Will sit up high
And watch the paddy

9. Husking pedal falls,
cow delivers
Oven burns
Fine paddy, black child
May I stay married forever.

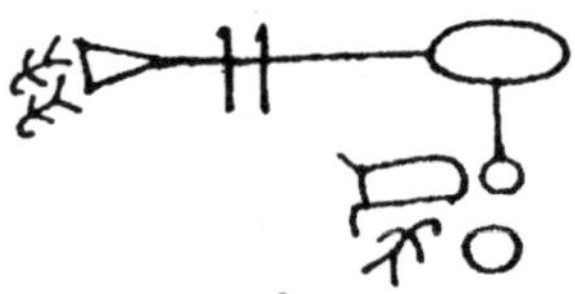

10. Bed of comfort, bolsters strewn
Beauty, youth, love all around

11. Worship as I a rice-paste kitchen
May I have a real, good one.

12. I worship a rice-paste cowshed
May I have a real one.

13. Kids in arms, kids all over.

14. Prayer for a brother.

15. Ripe paddy, banana
My husband Narayana
To war he will go
Return safely, I hope

16. Prayer for husband

Kin's wife, daughter and
daughter-in-law
May I be, as I pour
Honey and ghee.

17. Prayer for husband

18. Dad's become emperor
Brother the king
May wishes come true
O betel-nut tree.

19. The rhyme wishes
co-wives to die of burning.

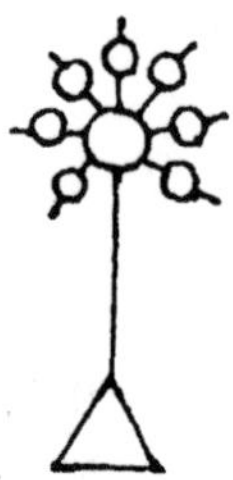

20. Another rhyme against co-wives

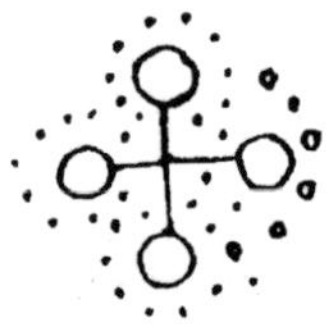

21. Custard-apple and deity
(May I) Have vermillion on
head, lac-dye on feet.

22. Sandalwood and Ghee
Clean clothes for the night.

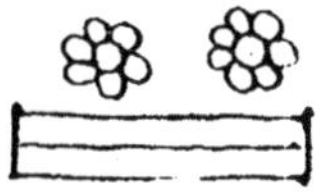

23. A wooden seat for my brother.

24. Light from a lamp, as she
prays for light for the world.

25. Worship the vermillion cask
Eat from gold plates.

26. Same as above

27. O Lord, may my husband
Be king of all.
May co-wives be servants
And I visit parents once
A year.

28. Move, move, my brother is
The bridegroom
What he spits out
Others eat.

29. Same as above

30. I paint paan tray with rice-paste

31. O conch-shell
May my father be a king
Brother a badshah.

32. May I have
Husband like Rama
Be chaste like Sita
Brother-in-law like Lakshman
Father-in-law like Dasarath
Mother-in-law like Kaushalya
Sons like Kunti
Be a cook like Draupadi
Enjoy love like Durga
Be humble as durba (a kind of grass).

33. Bird, bird, bird
May I sit and watch
Co-wife taken for burning

34. Mynah, mynah, mynah
Co-wives no more please

35. Bird, bird, May I
Be happy always.

36. *Arsi, Arsi, Arsi* (mirror)
May husband learn Farsi (Persian).

37. *Hata, hata, hata* (ladle)
Eat co-wife's matha (head)

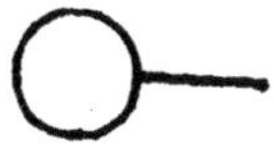

38. *Beri, Beri, Beri* (hand cuff)
Co-wife's a cheri (demon)

39. Mongoose go away
Save my husband, eat the co-wife

40. Worship Indra, sister of seven brothers
May I have children and paddy
Stay married till last.

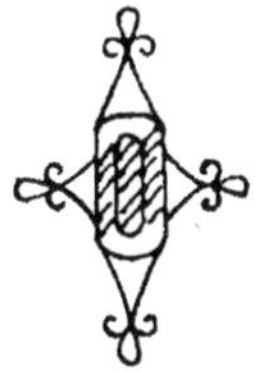

41. Pie for parents,
Pie for in-laws
Pie for my husband

42. Go and search nice husband
for me.

43. With a waist like this
May I enjoy my husband's love

44. May what I paint with rice-paste
Come true in life.

45. Let co-wife die and life be as mice
As the babui (a small bird) nest on
a date-palm tree.

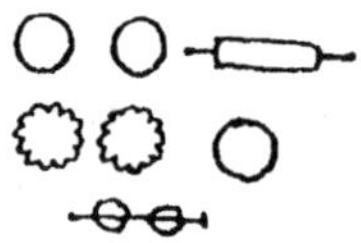

46. I paint rice-paste ornaments
So may I have real ones

47. Co-wife be a barren women

48. Bamboo shoots and beauty
Father as king, brother his
Subject

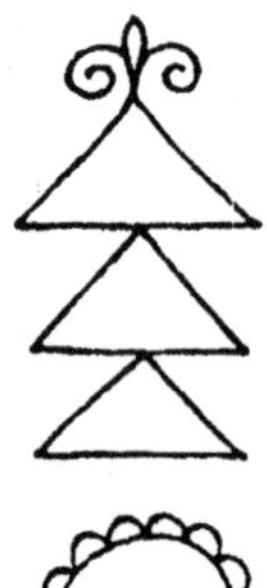

49. Honey, ghee and sugar cane
May I be a king's daughter and
another's woman.

50. As I paint rice-paste bangles
So may I have gold ones

51. Grandson what kept you,
Mohour in sacks had to be kept
Paddy in sacks had to be weighed
Rice in sacks had to be stored
Pulses in sacks had to be kept.

52. Oh my Lord,
the other person sleeps
here and there,
Let me have a golden cot.

Sandhyamani Brata: Observed on the last day of Kartick, the seventh month in the Bengali calendar, it continues during the whole of the next month, *Aghrayan.* In the evening the woman has to sit with a pitcher of water and stare at the sky. When one star appears she has to make a circle and she cannot speak until five stars are seen. Then the prayers for the welfare of brothers and husbands is chanted five times and the ingredients like flowers, grass, paddy, thrown in the water.

Mushkil Asan Brata: Actually a worship of *Vishnu* to get rid of troubles. Only Brahmin women can observe such a *brata* after cooking and eating eight fistful of rice with some green vegetables but nothing fried. Also she is not supposed to waste even a single grain of rice.

Ghentu Brata: For curing skin diseases as the juice of the ghetu leaf (a plant that grows widely) is supposed to have medicinal properties. There are other such *bratas* for curing diseases, like *Sitala* for small-pox, *Olaichandi* for cholera, *Champak Chaturdasi* for tuberculosis.

Nakhchhut Brata: As the name suggests, the cutting of nails (*nakh*) by a female barber has a major role to play in the observance of this ritual. It is observed in four consecutive years, the number of women invited, all married, going up from four to sixteen. On the final year the barber cuts off the nails of the women and also the *brati*, ties these up in a small bundle which the *brati* immerses in a pond after thrice asking whether her nails and flesh have been taken care of to which the barber replies in the affirmative. The prayer is for a rosy complexion, body like honey container, small feet and face like the moon.

Sivaratri Brata: Considered the best among the rituals, performed for the fulfillment of every desire that a woman can have. Men can also perform it for getting rid of their sins. Belief has it that Mahadeva had told Parvati of this when she had wanted advice on a ritual which everybody could perform. Mahadeva told her he would be *immensely* satisfied with those who would perform this *brata* on a dark moonless night in the month of *Falgun*. Those observing it would have to take vegetarian food the day before, sleep on a bed of straw taking Mahadeva's name, collect bel leaves after bathing early the next morning and in the night worship clay idols of Siva, in the first hour with milk, in the second with curd, in the third with clarified butter and with honey in the fourth. They will have to stay awake the whole night and the next morning feed Brahmins and give them money before eating themselves.

According to mythology, Mahadeva had told Pravati the story of a hunter in Varanasi who had worshipped Shiva without knowing that he was doing so and so Siva had stood by him when Yama's men had come to take him away. A satisfied Parvati told the saints about the *brata* and they spread its message throughout the world.

Yampukur Brata: Performed by unmarried women for the prosperity of parents. A hole is dug to represent the pond of Yama, around it are planted saplings, idols of the deity, his wife and aunt are placed on the southern side and those of birds and aquatic animals like sharks, crocodiles and tortoise are thrown in the water filled hole.

The tale of the *brata* is about an old woman, her son Sukhraj, daughter Dugraj and her daughter-in-law. Her daughter-in-law used to worship Yama every year and on each occasion she used to spoil it. This though Dugraj was married to Yama himself. Then one day the woman died and after some time Yama told Dugraj never to go southwards. One day she did that and saw her mother being beaten up by Yama's men. When she asked Yama the reason for this she was told her mother was paying the price for spoiling her daughter-in-law's worship of Yama. She then went to her sister-in-law and at her chest the latter again worshipped Yama and the mother-in-law was saved from her tortures in hell.

Sasthi Brata: Sasthi is the deity with whose blessings children are born and who also looks after them. No rural woman dares to annoy her and she is worshipped on every full moon night of the year. For each month the ritual has a different name, such as *Dhula Sasthi* in Vaisakh to protect children from dust (*dhula*), *Aranya Sasthi* in the next month for protecting them from death. In the month of *Asvin*, pregnant women observe Durga Sasthi as the deity Durga herself is believed to have worshipped Sasthi during this month.

Sasthi Brata.

There are many tales narrated at the time of observance of the different Sasthi *bratas*. The most popular is the one associated with *Aranya Sasthi* or *Jamai Sasthi*. It runs as follows (collected from Mymensigh):

There were two friends, a milkmaid and a Brahmin woman. One day in the month of Jaistha an astrologer came to the house lead of the milkmaid and asked her to observe Aranya Sasthi *brata.* She agreed and asked her friend to also observe it as it would lead to good results. The Brahmin woman objected saying the custom was not prevalent in her community but ultimately both made arrangements for the *brata.* Sixty clusters each of bananas, mangoes, jackfruit, sixty baskets of puffed rice, parched rice, sixty pots of curd and other things were procured. Then the Brahmin woman told her daughter-in-law to look after the things while she and her friend went to the river for their bath.

The daughter-in-law was greedy. Left alone she collected a plantain leaf, put bits of everything on it and ate these. On her return the mother-in-law could not find out what had happened but the deity, Sasthi, knew. The two friends observed the *brata* in their homes but the daughter-in-law stayed away.

Disaster then struck the family. The daughter-in-law gave untimely birth to a dead child and so did the cow and other pet animals in the house. The Brahmin woman thought it was all because she had broken a custom and observed the *brata* but her friend consoled her saying that with the blessings of the deity she would get back everything.

A year passed and next Jaistha again the same thing happened in her house. The daughter-in-law again ate the offerings before the *brata* was observed, again gave birth to a dead child and so did the animals. This went on year after year for six years.

On the seventh year the milkmaid suggested that this time her friend observe the *brata* in her house. Though unwilling the latter ultimately agreed. Before going for the ritual both the Brahmin woman asked her husband this time to guard the offerings. He agreed.

The daughter-in-law was in a fix. She was dying to eat the offerings but her father-in-law was there. She tried to get him away by various means but he remained at his post. After the *brata* was observed, the Brahmin woman looked for her daughter-in-law and found her lying with her tongue out. She drove her out after tying a roll of string used at the *brata* to her sari end, and telling her she would not get a son till the roll fully unwinds itself.

The daughter-in-law reached a locality inhabited by untouchables (*Chandalas*). There the string finally unwound itself and a boy was born. The daughter-in-law named him Govinda of Sasthi. When Yama came to take away the son, the daughter-in-law who had stolen Sasthi's food told him he could not take him as this time she had not committed any offence.

Govinda grew up into a fine child, started visiting houses and even that of the mother of Yama. One day the mother cried out in pain from a boil on her back and said she would bless anybody who would cure her with a son. Govinda's mother heard this, bit away the boil and told Yama's mother not to forget her promise. She saw it was the thief who had cured her but then she had already promised. The daughter-in-law returned to her in-laws' place with Govinda.

Govinda, however, wanted to visit Yama's mother and again went to her place and was told the only way he could come back was if he got his mother to repeat the same kind of theft. She taught the boy ways in which he could tempt his mother but he could not as she had accompanied him as a fly and heard everything. This continued for long but the daughter-in-law could not be tempted any more. Then, pleased with her, Yama's mother gave her the six sons who had died at birth along with a lot of wealth and they lived happily from then. People saw this as the power of Sasthi and from that day she began to be worshipped.

In some houses the story does not end there. They also speak of the milkmaid who had been blessed with a lot of children by Sasthi and whom she constantly abused for creating a ruckus in the house. So Sasthi decided the time had come to teach her a lesson. The deity made her do things on the day of the *brata* which she should not have done and lost everything and her children.

Meanwhile Govinda's friendship with Yama's mother had continued and he would learn from her why people suddenly suffered and what they should do to get rid of their troubles. When the milkmaid came to him to know what wrong she had committed he told her and said that the curse would lift if she put drops of curd made twelve years ago on everybody's eyes. Fortunately the milkmaid had such curd, did as she was told and got back her children and everything else.

Nilkul Vasudeva Brata: The narration shows that men also have a role to perform in *bratas.* It is believed that if a woman listens to the narration with betel leaves and betel nuts in her hand she would hear from her father, husband and son who live in distant places.

The tale is of a king who had shown disrespect to Nilkul Vasudeva even though his family had earned the kingdom by the deity's grace. By the deity's curse the king got separated from his queen, the queen from her sons who were brought up by the chowkidar of a village in another kingdom of which that king had become become the ruler. The queen was forced by a trader to accompany him on a river voyage but could not touch her as she had pleaded to the Sun god to make her a leper with the promise that when the time came her beauty would return.

After twelve years the boat came to that village and the chowkidar was asked by the king to guard it. Instead he sent the two boys to do so and there the leper woman, who was their mother, saw them. Without revealing her identity she asked them to meet the king who realised that they were his sons. The chowkidar, however, protested and at that stage the queen appeared to reveal her identity. The family was happily reunited and the chowkidar and his wife also lived with them for the rest of their lives.

In the *brata katha*, the story is narrated by a stupid Brahmin who had become wise and who travelled from one place to another telling people of the powers of Nilkul Vasudeva.

Madhu (Honey) or Sweets related Brata: Observed first in the last day of *Chaitra* and continues for a year, the rituals performed in the last day of each month. Brahmins are needed, their number going up every month. On the first month the Brahmin is given sweets etc to bring out the desire to be hospitable.

Satyanarayan Brata: Observed on the day of full moon, either in the evening or just before it. The principal ingredient is 'sinni', a mixture of what flour, sweets, bananas etc. Five sets of offerings are made of betel-leaves, betel-nuts, bananas, molasses and some coins and are given to five Brahmins. These are called 'Mokam'. The *brata* is observed for prosperity, peace in the family and general wellbeing. This is a very popular *brata* in Bengali homes.

Baramahar Brata: Observed by Ho tribals to prevent evil spirits from harming domestic animals and poultry. In the evening of the *brata* they come out of their homes with sticks and making a lot of noise go to the jungle where below a tree the ritual is performed. A hen is marked with vermillion and let loose in the jungle, to represent fleeing evil spirits. The next day chickens are sacrificed and eaten together with 'haria', the liquor they brew at home.

Subachani Brata.

Subachani Brata: No fixed time for observance, can be observed throughout the year, to mark any happy occasion. Pitchers, mango leaves, lotus, small sweet balls, betel-leaf, banana, betelnuts, sesame, vermillion and rice-paste for the alpana painting are needed.

The story is about a poor woman and her son who one day wanted to eat meat and killed a lame duck belonging to the king. When the latter came to know what had happened be ordered the son to be imprisoned.

The grief-stricken mother did not know what to do when she heard of Subachani. She worshipped the deity and promised to keep on worshipping her if her son returned safe. The deity appeared in the king's dream and ordered him to release the son and get his daughter to marry him if he did not wish to be destroyed. The king did so, the son returned home with his wife and master of half the kingdom and the worship of Subachani became a regular event.

Nataichandi Brata: Observed more in the Dhaka, Faridpur areas of Bangladesh. The ritual is first observed in the first Wednesday of *Aghrayan*, then on every Wednesday of the month for four years. On the last year a grand feast is organized.

The *brata* is also observed in West Bengal but with a difference in that it is a Sunday ceremony. The *bratini* fasts the whole day and in the evening performs the ritual which in West Bengal is known as the *Nataimangalchandi Brata.*

The tale of the *brata* also differs in the two countries. The West Bengal version is:

There was a merchant who took a second wife on the death of the first who had given birth to two children. When the time came for him to sail abroad for his business he requested two friends to take care of the children if their foster-mother ill treated them. This was exactly what happened and after some time the foster-mother got information of the merchant's friends looking after the children and stopped them from doing so. One day the children were grazing the cattle and fell asleep out of hunger and on waking up found the cows gone. They were scared to return home and found shelter in another house and told the lady there of their problem. She got them to worship Nataichandi and with her blessing they got back the cows the next day.

Meanwhile the merchant had returned with a lot of wealth and hearing that the children had not returned home set out to find them. His greedy wife thought she would hide the wealth in the well, fell down and died. The merchant found the children and they spent their days happily thereafter.

The Bangladesh version is about a king who was worried about his children whom he had to leave in the care of their foster mother. Here also the children were made to worship Nataichandi one of the purposes of which is to bring home friends who were away. After they had done so, the king returned and hearing everything did away with his queen. His daughter, the princess, got married and had to go through further or-deals but Nataichandi always came to her aid and solved her problems.

Nirakali Brata: This *brata* can be observed every evening just after sunset. Men are not allowed but those who are willing to eat a whole betel-leaf can have a share of the offering made to the deity. Like all deities Nirakali is very particular about how she is worshipped and the slightest mistake can bring down her wrath on the worshippers or *bratinis*. On the other hand if she is pleased she is genorosity personified.

The story is of a princess who was not the only person not to be gobbled up by a she-demon who attacked her father's place. She tried to drown herself but was saved by the deity Nirakali who had chosen her as the preacher of her qualities. The princess heard a voice from heaven which said her troubles would be over if she worshipped Nirakali with a bunch of betel-leaves, betel-nuts, catachu and tobacco leaf. She was wondering where she would get these things from when king Dhananjoy saw her and married her. To him she said about the oracle and began worshipping the deity every day.

One day, however, she forgot and the curse of the deity came on her. The king lost everything in the game of dice and left for the forests with his queen and son. They reached a country where the king had just died and the people were looking for a successor. Seeing Dhananjoy and his royal bearing they took him to be the king and because of the deity's curse he forgot all about his queen and son.

The queen had to go through further hardships but ultimately the deity decided to help her and all problems ended. Dhananjoy remembered her and took her and the children to his new palace where she built the deity's place of worship and paved it with gold.

Ghātkāli Brata: The *bratini* tells the story of the ritual standing on the banks of a river or pond (*ghāt*) while others listen. The ingredients are the same betel-leaf, betel-nuts, catechu and tobacco leaf. One of the purposes is to ensure quick return of the husband who works away from home.

The story is of a merchant's son who, together with his wife and son, were living on the wealth left behind by his dead merchant father. One day, however, he had realised he had to earn on his own and so went on a journey leaving his wife and son with his maternal uncle giving him money for their food for six months.

He, however, did not turn up for two years and his wife began to be tortured by the maternal uncle's wife even though they were very wealthy. One day she decided to put an end to her life but heard an oracle that her problems would be over if she worshipped the deity Ghatkali. She was told of the ingredients and how she must get other women to listen to the story. With great difficulty she managed to get the ingredients and invited other women but the maternal aunt refused to come for which she was severely punished by the deity. Her husband also returned a wealthy man but was drowned as the woman had not promised to continue observing the ritual. She did that and the husband returned to life.

Sampad Brata: The Sampad *brata* is observed throughout the month of Vaisakh at two in the afternoon for peace in the family, prosperity and for avoiding widowhood. After the ritual is over the *bratini* says,

Son swings on the lap of my husband
May I die on the banks of the Ganga

The tale which is then narrated runs as follows:

The king and queen were playing dice. The king was losing and the queen was wining. The queen asked for a palace, the king got up, called his men, got a large and a small pond dug, a garden made and a house built. Then called out that the palace was ready. The queen went with her 16 companions found the ponds without water, no flowers or fruits in the garden and no noise of elephants and horses in the palace. She got angry and lay down. When the king wanted to know what had happened, she said, "do you called that a palace"? The king went to take a look again called his men. Water came in the ponds, flowers and fruits in the trees, peacocks danced, elephants and horses began to make noise. Next he asked the queen to take a look, she went with her companions, bathed in the ponds, plucked flowers and worshipped the deities. Then she asked,

All companions are happy
Why aren't you my Brahmin friend.

The companion replied that for 12 years she had not seen her husband and son who had gone to a distant land and so she could not make merry. The queen told her to observe her *brata* next *Vaisakh* and her husband and son would return.

Next *Vaisakh* the queen called her and asker her to make threads of cotton and listen to the tale of Sampad for 30 days. On the last day she would have to make 90 pieces of sweets of dried milk (*khir*), 90 pieces of *paan* (betel leaves), cut 90 betel nuts and same number of bananas from the tree. Thirty sweets should be given to Ganga, thirty to the priest and 30 she should eat. The companion did as she was told, gave sweets to Ganga and priest and as she bit into one of her own, her neighbours called out, "there come your husband and son". She dropped the sweet on the plate, spat out what was in the mouth, rubbed off her vermillion mark from the forehead, dirtied her sari, turned round and wept.

Came my son and went away
Came my husband and went away

Meanwhile the queen had sent her maid to find out about the *brata*. She returned and said that the companion was cursing both her and the *brata* itself. The queen went to her and found that the companion had not done as she had been told, had moved while eating the sweet. She asked her to observe the *brata* again next year.

The next year when the time for the *brata* came again, the companion asked the queen for one of her 16 jewel for offering to the deity. The queen did not agree but sent her maids to the king for his advice. The king was also reluctant to part with it but then it was a Brahmin girl asking for it and so gave his consent. Disaster struck his family, his elephant and houses died, his grains vanished. The king and queen set out from their home with two horses, two sons, a casket of ornaments and an umbrella. Wind took the umbrella, a kite stole the casket, sons were drowned while drinking water from the river and the horses died while grazing in the forest. The queen told they king the should go to her sister.

There they were well received but Sampad Narayan (deity of wealth) said,

Give jewel to another
Shouldered other's problem
Now have come to destroy sister's wealth

One day the sister placed gems before them which turned to ashes as they looked at those. The sister blamed them for stealing her gems and threw them out. The king said,

I had told you my queen
Gave our own to another
Shouldered her sorrow

The tale goes on to say how the two went through many privations, always received well at first and then thrown out. Ultimately they became servants of a prostitute. Then came the month of *Vaisakh*, the king asked the queen to observe the *brata*, with great difficulty they procured the ingredients and the rituals were performed. Now at last the deity Sampad Narayan was appeased and the royal couple got back everything. The queen went to her companion and told her,

Companion my companion
Return my jewel, take your troubles

The elephants, horses, grains returned. The gardens were once again full of flowers and the ponds got filled with water.

10

Brata : District-wise Observance

Sukhbhanta Brata: Common in South 24-Parganas. Observed at dawn on Kali Puja day by married and elderly women. Offerings to various deities are placed on two cowdung heaps round which a rice-paste border is drawn. The offerings are, raw bananas, pieces of sugarcane, betel-nuts etc. Candles or lamps are lit and the women lock up at the vesper and chant, 'happiness, happiness', while putting vermillion and grass on the mounds. Jute stalks are lit and in the morning cows are bathed after putting oil and vermillion on their horns. The ritual is for the family's welfare as well as that of the cattle.

Banbibi and Dakshinroy: The Royal Bengal Tiger is known as *Dakshinroy* (lord of the south) in the marshy areas of South 24-Parganas and also *Banbibi* (mistress of the forest). The worship takes place on the last day of *Chaitra* for protection from wild animals.

Manikpir: The deity of cattle, *Manikpir* is worshipped for their welfare. The ritual is conducted by a Maulvi of the Muslim

WEST BENGAL

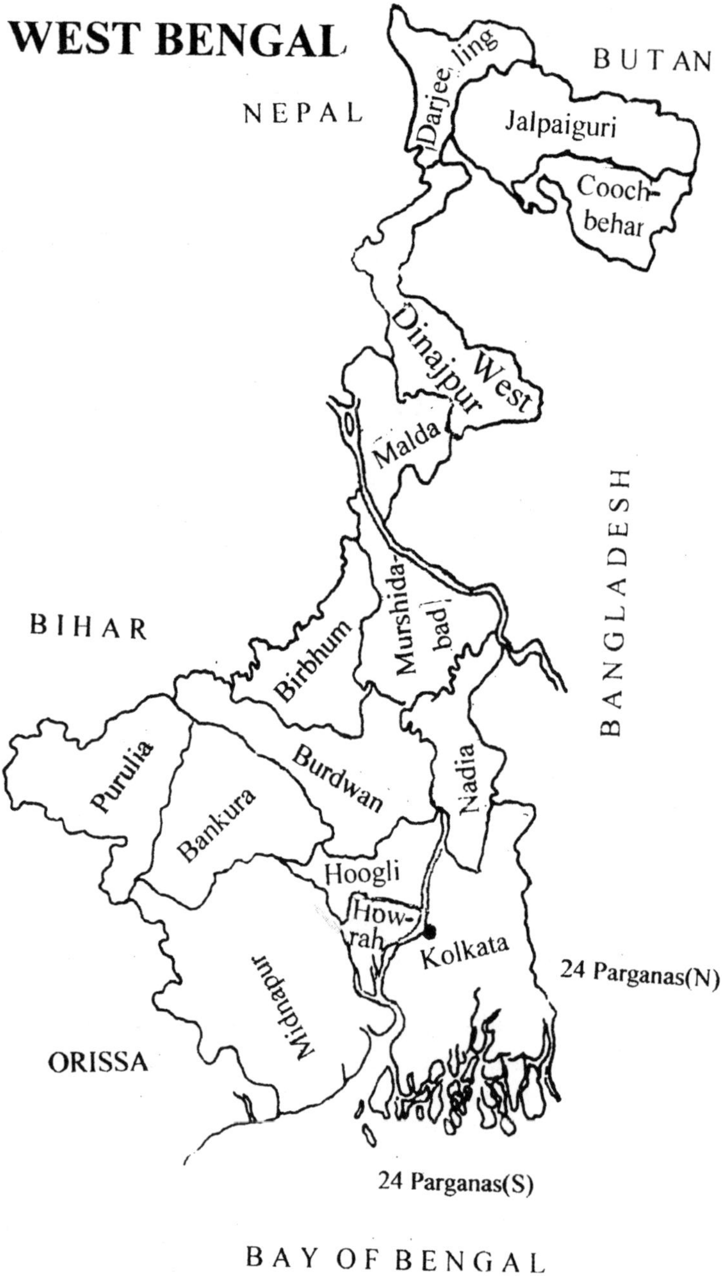
NEPAL
BUTAN
Darjee ling
Jalpaiguri
Cooch-behar
Dinajpur West
Malda
BANGLADESH
Murshida-bad
BIHAR
Birbhum
Purulia
Bankura
Burdwan
Nadia
Hoogli
How-rah
Kolkata
24 Parganas(N)
Midnapur
ORISSA
24 Parganas(S)
BAY OF BENGAL

community and is a fine example of communal harmony. The deity is popularly visualised as one with white complexion, flowing hairs, large eyes, prayer beads in hand as also a fly-whisk.

Arandhan: Observed on the last day of the month of *Bhadra* for good fortune and protection against snakes. *Manasa*, the deity of snakes, is worshipped and this continues throughout the month. There are two forms, one which says the ritual must be performed on Tuesdays and Saturdays and the other on the last day of the month. The latter insists that a preparation of edible roots, the hilsa and prawn be cooked which is eaten the next day by family members and relations.

In other parts of West Bengal the ritual is observed on the last day of *Shravana*, the month preceding *Bhadra*.

Shilnora Puja: The 'shilnora' or grinding stone is worshipped on the day after Saraswati Puja. The ritual involves eating vegetables cooked whole without salt and turmeric on the night before. On the next day, the day of the ritual, this is eaten with watered rice, oil and salt.

Briksha Puja.

Briksha Puja: Briksha means the tree, many varieties of which are to be seen in the Sunderbans in South 24-Parganas. There is a practice of marrying one tree with another, particularly the banyan with the peepul. Saplings of the two trees are planted, the normal marriage rituals are gone through and both watered throughout the dry month of *Vaisakh*. It is believed the woman who performs the ritual will be blessed with children. In some areas the ritual is observed in the month of *Aghrayan* when a growth of betel-leaves is worshipped. This is known as the *Latai Chandi Puja*. Some women also observe the *Dhelai Chandi*, which means tying a small piece of earth (*dhela*) to a date-palm tree and worshipped to cure children of nagging habits.

Ghentu Brata: To cure diseases, particularly of the skin. On the last day of the month *Falgun*, the ghentu idol is made of cowdung with cowrie-shell as eyes. Medicines for skin disease are distributed at night.

Ateswar Puja: A highly popular deity in South 24-Parganas who looked after cattle and other domestic animals. If a cow or goat is lost, the deity is worshipped with *ganja* (Indian hemp) and *batasa* (sweet drops of sugar or molasses).

Poush Parvana: Various deities are worshipped on the last day of *Poush* and the next day, the first of the month of *Magh*, with sugar, *batasa*, *ganja* and liquor.

Makal Brata: For the protection of boatmen and fishermen in the riverine South 24-Parganas. Two earthen mounds are worshipped next to a pond with vermillion.

Basanta Buri Brata: Like the *Sitala* worship this is also for protection against small-pox. The *brati* has to fast the whole day and worship a pot on which a green coconut is placed after it is washed with the water of another.

In this district betel-leaf growers worship *Pavana*, the deity of wind, to protect them from storms and *Olaichandi* is worshipped as a protection against cholera.

Thakthaki Brata: Once popular in Nadia, now almost extinct. Performed by elderly women to keep away cholera and other diseases. In Howrah there is the *Betai Chandi Brata* for the family's welfare and *Pati Durga Mata Brata* in Hooghly for getting children.

Birinchi Brata: Birinchi is the deity of birth and worshipped in Midnapore district on all four Sundays of the month of *Poush*. The song of the ritual says, "Whosoever worships Birinchi or listens to the song, Is blessed with children". It also advises barren women to perform the ritual for four years with milk and fruits.

Baluka Brata: Observed by unmarried girls of Midnapore for a happy married life, in the seventh month of *Kartick*. Fresh milk and peas are offered to idols made by them of sand or mud. The ritual lasts for five days and on the sixth day the idols are immersed.

Bhēnpu Brata: Observed in the tribal areas of Bankura in the moonless nights of *Kartick* and *Aghrayan*. There is no idol of the deity. A cowdung mud is prepared, smeared with oil and vermillion and on it a pot is placed filled with water and with mango leaves and branches of banyan tree on top. The offerings are pies made of powdered rice, clarified butter and molasses. Men cannot be a part of the ritual or even share the offering. The *Bhēnpu* is essentially a deity for child birth but is also worshipped by some to get back lost cattle.

In Bankura, *Mahadona Devi* is worshipped for protection of crops and *Baghrai Brata* observed for protection against floods and excessive rain.

In Birbhum the *Baba Kudro Buro Brata* is observed for curing the sick.

Vana Beruno Brata: Ritual observed in Murshidabad by women to keep away epidemics of cholera and small-pox. Performed on three consecutive days in the month of *Chaitra* when clay dolls resembling domestic animals are worshipped. Before beginning the ritual the woman has to cut her nails, eat vegetarian food and fast during the three days it is performed. During this period she also has so stay inside her room and cannot do such normal chores as washing her clothes or boiling paddy.

Musafir Brata: Jointly performed by Hindus and Muslims of Murshidabad for the stoppage of rain. A male figure is made of old clothes and two bags are hung from its hands into which people drop rice and pulses. These then are cooked and eaten by all.

Meleni Brata: Observed in Murshidabad by little girls, the purpose being to ensure happy married life in future. A six-inch clay idol is made and washed in a water filled hole. Performed throughout the month of *Chaitra* when the girls dress the idol in many ways and offer it sugarcane molasses, milk, sweets and fruits as also vegetables in some places. *Meleni* is also a deity of fertility which is evident from the things offered to her.

Bhanjo Brata: Observed by backward castes and tribals in north-west Burdwan, south Birbhum and Murshidabad districts. Of late men are also participating in it. The ritual is performed on eight consecutive evenings, starting with the eleventh day of the lunar fortnight (*ekadasi*), and the deity is immersed on the morning of the ninth day. The ingredients are *chura* (flattened rice), curd, milk, sweets, nine types of fruits etc. The deity is placed at an elevated position, lamps are lit and songs sung.

Before the commencement of the ritual, a goat is sacrificed or some paddy seeds are kept on a designed vessel. If the seeds do not sprout then more songs are sung to please the deity *Bhanjo*. The theme is fertility, both of the women performing the ritual and the land.

Karam Gusain Brata: The ritual is observed both by upper castes and tribal girls and women. On the day of the ritual, unmarried girls cover a vessel with sand or mud and sprinkle an uneven number of seeds on it, on which is sprinkled turmeric water and kept at some high place. Every morning and evening more such water is sprinkled to help the seeds sprout. This goes on till the time of immersion when in some villages animal sacrifices are made.

This is essentially tree worship and the theme is fertility. It is also observed in Bihar, Orissa and the present Jharkhand. On the one hand it symbolises a synthesis of tribal culture with that of the lower caste Hindus as also a synthesis of the cultures of neighbouring states.

Bhadu Brata: Another ritual observed in West Bengal's borders with other states through which unmarried girls express their desires. An idol of *Bhadu* is made and they sing her arrival song. The story of the *brata* has a princess being transferred into Bhadurani and the ritual is observed throughout the month *Bhadra*, fifth in the Bengali calendar.

Karam Brata: Ritual of women belonging to such tribal communities as Santhal, Oraon and Birhor of Midnapore and Purulia districts. The purpose is to have good crops and the women observing it are called Parvati. A similarity can be noticed with the gardens of Adonis, the ceremonies intending to promote the growth of or revival of vegetation (James Frazer: *The Golden Bough*). Benoy Mahato has also found similarities between this ritual and those of Syria and Egypt where the idols are Attis, Tammujo or Adonis.

Go-Brata: Ritual performed by tribals to protect cattle from wild animals on Kali Puja night. The story says that when the land was even more dry, the cattle had refused to work as they did not get enough to eat. From his heavenly abode *Mahadeva* assured them he would come down to see their plight. On the night before he came the men gave the cattle a wash so that when he came he was deceived by the cattle and cursed them with eternal service to men. Since then looking after them has become a practice.

Tusu Brata: Another ritual worth mentioning in this region is the *Tusu.* It is observed during harvesting in the month of *Poush. Tusu* is the deity of good harvest and she is worshipped with great fanfare.

Purulia in this border region of the state sees many rituals being performed throughout the year. In *Jaistha,* the second month, is observed the *Joymangalbar* as well as the *Aranya Sasthi* for the welfare of children. On the 13th of the month is observed the *Rohiṇ Brata* for the protection of crops. *Ambubachi* and *Bipattarini* are the rituals for the next month Asadh. Then in *Sravana* are observed the *Lotao* or *Lunthansasthi Brata* and the *Khaichera Brata.*

A veriety of rituals are performed in North Bengal also. Some of these are:

Sanjha Brata: Observed in parts of Malda district by small girls. On the morning of the first day of *Aghrayan* a small altar is made for the deity and in the evening they sit round it and sing the songs of *Sanjha,* the prayer being essentially for good husbands. The fertility theme is also noticed here and the ritual has similarities with *Sanjpujni* and *Katayani bratas* of North Bengal.

Haat Ghurni: A ritual of Jalpaiguri district. Performed by women in the months of *Vaisakh* and *Jaistha* for rain and thus owes its origin to the ancient belief in the supernatural powers of prayers. The women go round the *haat* or weekly markets, carrying mixtures of rice and milk and as they make the 'ulu' sound by moving their tongues inside their mouths, the men beat drums and young boys dance. The ritual is also for deliverance from all evil.

Mechheni-Teesta Buri: A popular all women ritual of Jalpaiguri. Groups are formed, led by an elderly woman who is named 'Marwani'. A clay idol of *Teestaburi* is made and kept on a vessel and covered with a white cloth. The women take this to the place where the guarding deity of the village is suppposed to reside. Then begins the singing and begging of alms with which the ingredients for the ritual are bought. After the ritual the idol is immersed and the women have a feast.

Teesta is the river of Jalpaiguri and the ritual's name and manner suggest a close link between river and women, the one giving birth to crops and the other to children.

Shat Brata: A variation of *Sasthi Brata* for getting children and their welfare.

Kulo-Namano Brata: Observed in *Vaisakh* for bringing rain to the parched land. A *kulo* or winnow is placed in the middle of the courtyard and women sing and dance round it. Then they carry it on their heads and visit the homes of neighbours. The song says:

> "O my sister queen of clouds
> Wash your feet and let the water drop.
> Small drops for small lands,
> To reach the knees in the big".

It resembles *Punyipukur* and other such rituals as also the *Kulo Ghat Brata* of the Muslims.

Manwantara Brata: Observed on a moonless Monday by Brahman and Rajbansi women of Cooch Behar. Early in the morning the *brati* must have her bath and then without talking to anybody wind a sacred thread seven times round a banyan tree. Lakshmi and Vasudeva are then worshipped at the base of the tree. The belief is that the ritual is a protection against ill-luck and untimely death.

Subachani Brata: Another Cooch Behar ritual for good fortune. Can be observed at any time of the year and usually when a newly married girl enters her in-laws' house. The ritual has provision for sacrifice of goats or pigeons. The ritual is observed in other districts and Bangladesh also.

Katyani Brata: Widely performed by girls in Cooch Behar for wish fulfillment. The main thing here is a pyramid shaped house built with branches of trees and covered with banana trunks. Inside an earthen lamp is lit. The ritual is held on the full moon night of *Kartick* and is repeated every hour for four hours. The ritual is observed for four or five years for the marriage of daughters.

Hudum Chuka: Hudum Chuka is the water god and is worshipped during long periods of dought. Women gather in a field outside the village, take off their clothes and dance. No man is allowed there. The ritual is a continuation of an ancient practice.

Deul Puja Brata: Married women of some prominent Brahmin families of Cooch Behar still perform this ritual in the month of *Magh* for peace and the family's welfare. A shrine or *deul* is made, worshipped and then immersed.

Bateswara Puja Brata: Throughout the month of *Magh*, unmarried girls of Cooch Behar worship *Bateswara* who is the guardian angel of the house. They chant prays for wealth and good health for all.

In *Vaisakh* the girls observe the *E kul O kul Brata* for getting the same man as husband in this life and the next.

Discussing the North Bengal *bratas,* Sushil Kumar Bhattacharya has said: "These rituals have evolved round

Chandi, Sasthi, Lakshmi and *Manasa* and are portions of our old folk-tales" (Sushil Kumar Bhattacharya: *Uttar Banger Loksahitya O Sanskriti*).

The Nepalese of Darjeeling are Hindu and at the same respectful of Buddhism and adherence to both faiths is noticed in their culture. The last day of each month is considered holy by them and is observed with Hindu rituals. Again on the moonless night of *Vaisakh* they observe *Matri Aumi* which is influenced by Buddhism and is in keeping with their matriarchal society. In *Bhadra* they observe *Kushey Aushi* which is a worship of the *Kusha,* a kind of grass considered holy. The women observe *Rishi Panchami* which is a worship of *Mahadeva.* They also observe *Bhai Tika* (Brother's Day) and *Siva Ratri.* The first is a sisters' prayer wishing their brothers a long life and the latter is a worship of Mahadeva and also Gautam Buddha which is held at the famed Mahakal temple in Darjeeling town.

While most rituals are observed throughout West Bengal, there are some which are restricted to particular districts. These are:

Howrah: Tush-tushli, Manasa, Siva *brata,* Sital Sasthi, Itu, Dhelafela, Olaichandi, Betaichandi.

Hooghly: Mangalchandi, Buriaranda (observed on the last day of Sravana), Bramachandi, Patidurgamata.

Burdwan: Toshla, Bhanjo, Bipattarini, Ghentu, Kartick *brata.*

Bankura: Karam, Bhēnpur *brata,* Jitashtami, Sankattarini, Go-*brata,* Dharma *brata,* Ambubachi.

Birbhum: Mangalchandi, Toshla, Baba Kudorburo.

Midnapore: Darpan Darsan (mirror watching, in the Contai region), Birinchi, Baluka, Bhim Puja.

Purulia: Bhadu, Jaymangalbar, Aranya Sasthi, Lotan Sasthi, Khaichera.

Malda: Sanjha, Kulo Namano, Shaat, Garsi.

Murshidabad: Meleni, Musafir, Vanberuno (Kandi region), Banger Biye (frog's wedding), Harircharan, Satyanarayan, Jitaastami, Jiyatkali, Thakthaki, Ma Dumni.

Nadia: Banbibi, Patal Phõr, Kulai Chandi, Khedai Thakur, Satya Pir, Gaji Pir.

North 24-Parganas: Siva Brata, Savitri, Ashokasthi, Kulai Chandi, Kaluroy, Dhelai Chandi, Basanta Buri, Panchananda, Basuli, Jarasur, Makal, Manik Pir, Gaji Pir, Pavan Devata.

South 24-Parganas : Arandhan, Poush Parvana, Kumir Puja (crocodile worship), Sri Panchami, Ateswar, Briksha Puja (tree worship), Shuk Bhanta, Basantaroy.

Jalpaiguri: Haat Ghurni, Teestaburi, Karam Gusain.

Cooch Behar: Katyani, Gudumchuka, Subachani, Bateswara, E Kul O Kul, Deul Puja.

Darjeeling: Sithichad, Gathey Mangal, Keshey Aushi, Rishi Panchami.

Some rituals of one region enjoy similarity with those of others. Like Vana Beruno with Sitala, Bhanjo of Burdwan, Birbhum with Dashera in Darjeeling, Vana Beruno with Thakthaki of Murshidabad, Shilnora of South 24-Parganas with Sitalsasthi of Hooghly, Arandhan of South 24-Parganas with Buriananda of Hooghly, Khai Dhara of Bankura with Patal Phõr of Nadia.

11

Brata : Other States and Neighbours

Expression of a woman's desires through rituals is to be found in other states of India also as also in the neighbouring countries of Bangladesh and Nepal. Some of these rituals are discussed here.

Assam

Rituals or *bratas* occupy a central position in Assamese culture and these are observed throughout the year.

Ambubachi: Performed by widows and menstrual women for three days from the seventh day of Asadh. Popular belief has it that during the three days of *Ambubachi*, mother earth has her period of menstruation and hence all agricultural work is suspended. Those observing the ritual eat only fruits and drink fresh milk.

In the Kamrup district, all temples remain closed during these three days and 'kumari' or unmarried girls stand in front of the doors of the temple at Kamakshya collecting donations

AFGHANISTAN
Indian claim
Srinagar
Chinese line of control
CHINA
Indus
PAKISTAN
Amritsar
Brahmaputra
NEPAL
NEW DELHI
Agra
Kānpur
BHUTAN
Imphāl
Ganges
Kāndla
Bhopāl
BANGLADESH
Ahmadābad
Calcutta
Haldia
BURMA
Nāgpur
Arabian Sea
Mumbai (Bombay)
Vishākhapatnam
Bay of Bengal
Hyderābād
Panaji
Marmagao
Chennai (Madras)
Andaman Islands
Bangalore
Pondicherry
Calicut
Port Blair
Cochin
Madurai
Tuticorin
Nicobar Islands
Laccadive Sea
SRI LANKA

from pilgrims. Giving this donation is a form of 'kumari' worship. On the fourth day the pilgrims are allowed to enter the temples and are blessed with a piece of red cloth, red being the colour of desire. The whole ritual seems to be related to the fertility theme.

Sivaratri: Observed in the month of *Falgun*. The *brati* has to fast the whole day and perform the ritual at every hour of the night.

The *Manasa* or *Maroi* ritual is also performed in Assam as a protection against diseases and also for wealth and children. Temple priests do the worship.

Tripura

The culture is a mixture of Hinduism and folk rituals. The royal family has embraced *Shaiva* and also *Vaishnav* faith but at the same have not forgotten their original practices, proof of which can be had in the *Kharchi Puja*, worship of fourteen deities, in the month of *Asadh*.

Most of the rituals of Tripura were brought into the state by Bengali Hindus from adjoining areas which are now part of Bangladesh. Some are also Muslim rituals.

Hari Parameswar Brata: Observed mainly in the northern parts, in the end of *Kartick* and beginning of *Aghrayan*. Thirty two small balls of rice, banana, sugar, coconut etc are made and the priest has to bring an equal number of clay pieces supposed to represent gold and silver. The ritual is a mix of Aryan and non-Aryan beliefs and is also a reminder of mythological tales.

Bhadra Chandi: Observed in the month of *Bhadra*. There is no idol of the deity who is worshipped on Tuesday. After the ritual is performed the *brati* eats rice with a vegetable preparation but the same vegetable cannot be eaten on consecutive Tuesdays. On the last Tuesday rice and curd is eaten. It is performed for the family's welfare.

Jhatpat Thakur: The ritual is performed only after the deity answers prayers by way of solving problems. The story is of a father who could marry of his daughters only with the blessings of Jhatpat Thakur who had visited him in the guise of a beggar.

Aula Kharini: Another ritual observed if the deity cures a family member of waywardness. It is observed on Tuesdays and Saturdays of any month.

Thanki Thakrun: Performed for wealth on any day with rice, bananas, fruits, sugar etc. Then the story of the ritual (*Brata Katha*) is told which is about how the deity came to the aid of a poor woodcutter who spread her fame in the village.

Kal Bhairab: Worshipped to prevent epidemics and famine. The deity, *Kal Bhairab,* is believed to be a discipline of *Siva* and the ingredients of worship are liquor and the tail portion of the Kalbosh fish (carp family).

Baghai: Believed to be a protection against tigers. It is observed in the month of *Magh,* from the 13th day to the end, not by women but by young men of a locality who collect donations by reciting rhymes composed by themselves. The donors are assured:

'Inside a fox's stomach
Shall go the tiger
in the forest'.

A tiger is made of a banana tree trunk and sacrified and the collected rice and pulses cooked and eaten.

Samaya Trani: Ritual observed to get rid of all dangers on Sunday and Thursday in the months of *Vaisakh, Aghrayan* and

Magh. The deity is represented by a pot before which the offerings, rice, banana, sugar, molasses drops, are placed lamps lit and the ritual performed with flowers and sandalwood paste. Stories are told of how the deity *Samaya Trani* repeatedly came to the aid of people in distress and saved them.

Byangeer Biye (Marriage of Frogs): To invite rains, vermillion marks are put on frogs to mark their 'marriage' and a rhyme is chanted. It is addressed to the clouds, both dark and white, who are requested to wet the earth below.

Garoi brata: Prevalent in West Tripura. The five sons of *Mangal Chandi, Fulkar, Nagkar, Jalkar, Sakalkar* and *Balaikar*, are worshipped along with their mother for a month from the last day of the month of *Chaitra*. The ritual is performed on every Tuesday of *Vaisakh* when fruits, sugar, parboiled rice, milk and molasses drops are offered. On the last day a number of families of the locality get together and a priest performs the ceremony. It is for domestic peace and welfare.

Chamar Jhee: Observed on Saturdays and Tuesdays, for curing diseases. The woman who performs the ritual and the ailing person have to fast from the morning. In the afternoon some rice is begged from the *Chamar* (low caste) community, which is pounded and mixed with bananas, sugar, fruits to make the offering for the deity.

Khawaj Pir: A Muslim ritual who believe that a living Pir or holy man resides under water who has to be appeased for the cure of dropsy and rheumatism. The deity is also believed to have the powers to save people from drowning.

Manik Pir: Ritual performed for protection of cattle from diseases. It is related to the *Gorakshanath Brata* observed for the same purpose.

Bholapora: Observed in the afternoon of the last day of *Kartick* for a good harvest. An effigy of the deity is made with

Kusa (grass) and from it are hung dead insects, entrails of fish, buds of paddy etc which is taken to a paddy field belonging to the family and set on fire. This is done to pray for the death of rats and insects which damage crops.

Maghdeswari or Maghini: Observed in South Tripura to appease the deity *Maghini* who is believed to cause diseases which no doctors can cure. A place away from the ailing person's house is cleared and there the red 'jaba' (Chinarose) and some black threads are put in a cage. Then vultures are invited and the ritual ends when one of these, the queen vulture, touches the patient or puts some grass in the palms which is worn as an amulet. The word *Maghini* has perhaps come from thc Buddhist Mogs who at one time made South Tripura their home.

Kaura-Kauri: Observed to cure persistent cough and cold. On any Saturday or Tuesday an offering of *Chura* (flattened rice), curds, flowers etc is placed under a 'Kau' (Gapcinia Cow) tree and a portion of this is eaten by the ailing person.

Kalkinarayan Brata: On any evening offerings have to be made in the courtyard to the deity. Five men are invited to smoke a particular hookah and then the tale of the ritual is recited. In a nutshell, it is about how a Brahmin twice got back his cow by worshipping the deity *Kalkinarayan.* The refrain is, 'Stolen treasures come back'.

Maghmandal: Worshipping the sun so that its rays destroy all germs. Observed by women throughout the month of *Magh* when braving the bitter cold they have a dip at dawn.

Another ritual for curing skin diseases and eye or ear problems is *Kamkhat Brata* when the deity *Kamkhatla* is worshipped. The ingredients include a preparation of eight vegetables and 36 fried pies.

Akulanir Brata: Ritual for removing poverty, can be observed on any Sunday or Thursday in the months of *Baishak,*

Jaistha, Sravana and *Bhadra.* The ritual is performed round the basil tree which is found in almost all rural Hindu homes.

Komai Brata: For protection against fire ravages, observed on the full moon night of the month of *Falgun.* Five vegetable preparations are made and a little of each offered to the deity and the rest eaten by the *brati* to break her fast. The offering is then buried in a hole filled with water.

Kshetra Brata: The deity is believed to be an incarnation of Lakshmi and is worshipped on any Saturday or Tuesday of *Aghrayan* or *Magh,* for good harvest. Some of the offerings have to be begged from other homes.

Udaymangal Brata: Like *Kshetra,* no idol is needed here and the women pray round the basil tree for fulfillment of their different wishes. Observed on five consecutive Tuesdays in five months from *Kartick* to *Falgun.* Apart from the usual offerings, leaves of different fruits, like mango, jackfruit as also betel-leaves and leaves of 'kachu' (an edible root) are given, one on each occasion. The *brati* has to eat the same vegetables on these Tuesdays and she cannot talk while eating nor can anybody else eat the same preparation.

Dhanya Punima Brata: A portion of the courtyard is cleaned with cow dung, a sapling of the banana tree is planted and at its base a pot is placed. On the other side of the sapling holes are dug and filled milk and water of green coconuts. The ceremony is performed by a Brahmin.

Ashta Lokpal Brata: A form of Sun worship, not much in vogue these days. Used to be performed for eight days in the month of *Aghrayan.*

Orissa

In Orissa the *brata* is known as Osha which have some similarities with the rituals of West Bengal and also many differences. These are performed mainly by women but in some men also play a role. Some of the rituals are mentioned below in accordance with the months in which these are performed.

Vaisakh: Chhatua Sankranti or Pana Sankranti, Akshay Tritiya.

Jaistha: Savitri, Rajo Sankranti.

Asadh: Rajo Sankranti (first day of the month).

Bhadra: Khudurkuni Osha, Janmashtami, Radhashtami, Budhoi Osha, Jitashtami. Kukkuti, Somnath, Sudasha, Bali Tritiya, Ganesh Chaturthi.

Asvin: Ananta Chaturdasi, Garvana Sankranti, Durga Sasthi, Kumar Purnima, Dwuti Bahan.

Kartick: Kartickshan, Jamai Sasthi, Nag Chowthi, Rai Damodar, Panchak.

Aghrayan: Punda Osha, Lakshmi, Kanjiamla.

Poush: Sambadashami, Makar Sankranti.

Nagh: Maghsaptami, Sudasha.

Falgun: Shiva Chaturdasi.

Chaitra: Chaiti Mangalbar Osha.

There are some rituals observed by girls, married women and also men, like *Ekadasi, Siva Chaturdasi, Maghsaptami, Janmashtami* etc. Some are observed by tribals in the hilly regions as also the plains tribals of Mayurbhanj. These are, *Bandona, Brata, Damodar brata, Akhanda Shikar Brata.* Some of the rituals are mentioned here.

Akshay Tritiya: Observed by farmers. It is the first day of farming and observed on the full moon on *Vaisakh*, Jagannath is the principal deity in Orissa and on this occasion wheels are made for his chariot as also of his brother Balaram and sister Subhadra. The day is considered auspicious and so work on house building or digging ponds begins then.

Khudurkuni Osha: Observed by unmarried girls in the month of *Bhadra* and till the end of the first year after marriage. The purpose is to get a good husband and the ritual is performed exactly when the moon is seen.

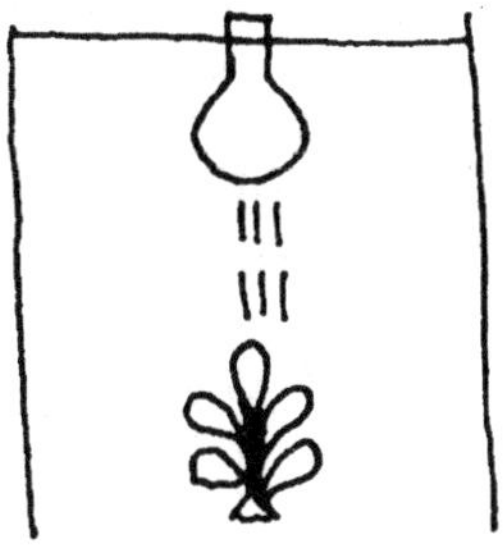

Chhatua Sankranti.

Chhatua Sankranti or Pana Sankranti: Observd on the first day of *Vaisakh* when both men and women eat *chhatu* (flour of barley or maize or pigeon pea) and drink sherbet made of the bel (wood-apple) fruit which is known as pana. It is the plead for fair distribution of rain during the dry months and is similar to the Basudhara Brata of West Bengal.

Kumar Purnima Brata: Young unmarried men and girls observe this on the Lakshmi Puja night in the month of *Asvin* and continue till the first year of marriage. Fruits betel-nuts, haritaki (myrobalan), mango leaves and sandalwood paste are needed. The participants hold hands and dance, singing songs to the moon.

Budhoi Osha: Budnoi Bamna is a regional deity and she is worshipped in the month of *Bhandra.* The deity gives sight to the blind, children to the barren women, cures lepers. The story is that by worshipping her the wife of a wine seller was cured of her leprosy and her five sons killed by a king, regained their lives. She is a vengeful deity and punishes those who forget to fast while worshipping her. In this she resembles Manasa of Manasamangal Kavya.

Ganesh Chaturthi: Ganesha is worshipped as the deity of knowledge during the moonlit nights of *Bhadra.*

Rai Damodar and Panchak Brata: Hindu widows observe this for twenty five days in the month of *Kartick.* The ritual is for the welfare of all and Lakshmi is worshipped along with Damodar or Krishna. The ritual has similarities with the *Baluka Brata* of adjoining Midnapore district of West Bengal.

Bihar

Rich in folk culture, many aspects of which are yet to be discovered, which still lives in songs, tales, proverbs, riddles etc. Some of the rituals according to the month of observance are:

Baishakh: Baisakhi Troyodashi

Jaistha: Batsavitir Brata.

Asadh: Sitala Brata

Sravana: Nagpanchmi, Jhoolan, Madhu Sravani Brata.

Bhadra: Teej, Ananta Chaturdashi, Barunisnan.

Asvin: Jeotia, Lakshmi Brata, Navaratri Brata.

Kartick: Chhat, Gopa Ashtami, Gangasnan, Kartick Purnima, Bhratridwitya Ahoi Asthami.

Aghrayan: Bibaha Panchami, Devotthan, Ekadasi.

Poush: Makar Sankranti, Nabanna.

Magh: Chautha, Basant Panchami, Magh Amaosh.

Falgun: Sivaratri.

Chaitra: Gouritritiya, Ram Navami, Chait Satuani, Sitala Ashtami, Chaitra Navami. Unmarried women worship trees on every Thursday wearing yellow coloured clothes.

Ahoi Asthami: A *brata* observed by married woman with children. It is observed for the welfare of husbands. At the beginning of the month of Kartick of the day of *brata* the woman, who have to fast the whole day, make eight types of dolls with buns on their heads and also paint pictures of children below the dolls. When the evening star is seen the ground is cleaned and a pot of water is placed on a wooden seat. The *bratini* then does her puja and listen to the *brata* katha. A special feature of this *brata* is that the *bratini* has to put on a silver necklece which is known as the 'Ahoi ornament.' The necklece is made of small pieces of silver and has a locket which the made attraction. The ingredients of the *brata* are rice and milk which are placed in front of the picture of Ahoi. Some money and halva are also kept in a separate utensil and *bratini* has to hold seven grains of wheat which listening to the *brata.* On completion of the *brata* the money and halva are given to the mother-in-law and the *bratini* breaks her fast after making offerings to the moon.

Teej: Observed by married women in the month of *Bhadra* during the moonless period. The ingredients are rice, *atta* (wheat flour), fruits which they eat on the morning after the ritual.

Makar Sankranti: Observed in the month of *Poush* for overall welfare.

Chautha Brata: Observed on the fourth day of the full moon *Magh*, by married women, for the welfare of children. Vermillion is smeared on two heaps of cowdung which are worshipped with the pictures of Ganesha and Lakshmi on either side.

Sivaratri Brata: Worship of Siva by both men and women three nights before the new moon in *Falgun.*

Chhat Puja: A major ritual in Bihar observed in the month of Kartick. On the day before the ritual, children build a small altar, the belief being that Sun will rule his kingdom from there. In the evening six or seven types of fruits are arranged in a vessel and clarified butter lamp lit. This vessel is bathed and offered to Sun. An essential part of the ritual is the sighting of sunset and sunrise. The main purpose of the ritual is getting children.

The mythological tale associated with the ritual speaks of a merchant who had gone blind because he had insulted the Sun God and in remorse wanted to commit suicide. He was, however, prevented by the sage *Narada* who advised him to perform the *Chhat* ritual, which he did and got back his eyesight.

The other tale is of an old woman who had got a son by the grace of Chhat Mata and promised to worship her. She, however, forgot to do so and the son died soon after marriage. As his newly married wife wept, *Chhat Mata* appeared, brought him back to life and said he had died because his mother had not kept her promise. The old women realised her mistake and observed the Surya Sasthi ritual from which was born *Chhat Puja.*

There are quite a few rituals in the Bhojpur area of Bihar. These are:

Chaitra: Gouri Tritiya.

Sravan: Nag Panchami.

Bhadra: Ananta Chhaturdeshi.

Asvin: Jeevat Puttika Brata.

Uttar Pradesh

Some of the rituals and the months when these are observed:

Chaitra: Chaitra Baruni, Mahashtami, Kamada Ekadasi, Navratri, Ramnavami, Arundhati, Ganagour, Chaitri Amabasya.

Baisakh: Akshay Tritiya, Mohini Ekadasi, Krishna Ekadasi, Ashmai, Akhateej.

Jaistha: Ganga Dusshera, Nirjala Ekadasi, Achala Ekadasi Barsait Amabasya.

Asadh: Vyas Purnima, Harishayani Ekadasi, Devshani Ekadasi.

Sravan: Kajari Purnima, Harishayani Ekadasi, Devshani Ekadasi.

Sravan: Kajari Purnima, Srabanshukla, Teej, Mangalagouri, Nagpanchami, Putrada Ekadasi, Pavitra Ekadasi.

Bhadra: Ganga Panchami, Magha, Ganga Navami, Govatsa Ekadasi, Ganesh Chaturthi, Surya Sasthi, Durba Ashtami, Anant Chaturdasi, Govatsa Dwadasi, Atri Ganga Navami, Probodhini Ekadasi.

Asvin: Jeotia, Vijaya Dashami, Ashoka Brata, Sarat Purnima, Indira Ekadasi, Navratri, Dusshera, Varaha Chaturdasi, Upanga Lalita.

Kartick: Karwa Chauth, Amla Navami, Tulsi, Ganga-Jamuna, Dhanteras. Deepavali, Annakut, Gopashtami, Kartick Purnima, Chandrayan, Akshay Navami.

Aghrayan: Dhanbrata, Mokshada Ekadasi, Utpanna Ekadasi, Champa Sasthi.

Poush: Makar Sankranti, Ghatpat, Pati Brata, Chiriamuthi, Bhagwanpat, Nanad Brata, Brahman Brata, Jethanbhet, Gajiabhar Brata.

Magh: Maunibrati Amabasya, Basant Panchami, Sitala Sasthi, Surya Saptami, Maghi Snan, Chouth, Ganesha Chaturthi.

Falgun: Mahasivaratri, Sitashtami, Janaki, Holika Dahan, Vijaya Ekadasi, Ashmata Brata, Shyamjee Brata.

Nagpanchami: Observed on the fifth day of the dark fortnight of *Sravana*, to worship snakes. There are two tales related to the ritual both saying how revengeful snakes ultimately helped women who prayed for them. On this day the field is not cultivated, no cooked food is eaten and milk is offered to snakes.

Somavati Amabasya: If the new moon falls on a Monday then it is observed by married women. Cows and trees (peepul particularly) are worshipped and oil is taboo.

Marudagna Brata: To be performed for a year from the new moon of *Aghrayan.* It is observed by all for the fulfillment of various desires. When the year ends, the women have to feed husbands and Brahmins.

Haripanchak Brata: Vishnu Worship. The woman has to take, milk, curd, clarified butter, cow's urine and honey before performing the ritual.

Masoprobas Brata: Can be performed in any of the three months of *Asadh*, *Shravana* and *Bhadra.* Widows and hermits can observe this ritual. The object is to attain nirvana.

Varaha Chaturdasi: God in his incarnation as *Varaha* (boar) is worshipped. The idea is to stay free of evil spirits and attain heaven.

Chandrayan Brata: A renowned ritual, it lasts for a month from *Kartick.* Fruits are consumed, the amount going up in equal measure for the first fortnight and declining in the same way in the next fortnight.

Narak Chaturdasi: Worship of Krishna in *Kartick* on the last day of the lunar fortnight, for attaining heaven.

Pradosh Brata: Observed mostly by men at sunset on the thirteenth day of any period. Shiva is worshipped for children. No restrictions on food.

Madhya Pradesh

A state rich in folk tales and the songs of roving mistrels. Some of the rituals, month-wise:

Chaitra: Gangour or Jawara, Fulpati, Ramnavami, Ashamata, Milimai, Dasamata.

Baisakh: Akhateej, Arwateej.

Jaistha: Barmatam, Gangadashami, Behrun Puja, Ghaila, Bidri.

Asadh: Devshani Ekadasi.

Bhadra: Karam, Bhojali, Krishnashtami, Bhaibeej, Rishi Panchami, Halchhat, Dol, Bajbaras, Anantchowdas, Kujalaya.

Asvin: Sanja Puja, Mamuylia, Bari Puja, Navratri, Garba, Ghadulia, Tisu Mata Puja, Dussehra, Nabanna.

Kartick: Dhanteras, Narkachowdos, Diwali, Gowardhan (Annakut), Gopashtami.

Poush: Chhetra, Haldi Kumkum, Makar Sankranti.

Magh: Ganesh Chaturthi, Vasant Panchami, Teej.

Falgun: Meghnad, Sivaratri, Bhagria, Holi, Jhanda, Pandum, Parad, Kokmar.

Hariri: Observed in the month of Sravan. Mainly a farmers' ritual who plant new crops on the day.

Kajri Navami: Also observed in *Sravan.* In the Western Ghats fishermen worship the sea with coconuts. Women decorate house with alpana paintings and this is known as Navami.

Karam: Tribals like Oraons, Baiga, Majhar observe this ritual during the rains in *Bhadra.* Three branches of the 'karam' tree are planted to represent their Karam Raja. Then the next day the branches are garlanded, rice and curd offered and girls roam the village with these. A post-harvest ritual.

Ganesha Chaturthi: Involves the worship of Ganesha and the Moon whose idols are made of cowdung. Through the ritual married women pray for the welfare of husbands and children. A mixture called 'pahar' is made of sesame and molasses and distributed after the ritual among friends and relations. If a pregnant woman misses the ritual one year she can nevertheless maintain continuity by getting another to distribute 'pahar'. The tale of the ritual has Siva announcing that every good work must start with the worship of Ganesha.

Teej: Wheat seeds are planted a fortnight or week before the ritual is observed, the day before Ganesha Chaturthi. When the seeds begin to sprout, women bathe and worship Shiva for the welfare of the family.

Harchhat Brata: Siva worship for the children's welfare. Women observing the ritual must husk the pady grown in their own land and eat that rice and rub their teeth with a branch like that of the banyan tree. The juice must not be swallowed but spat out.

Haldi Kumkum: Performed by married women. Small gifts are given to the invited women on whose foreheads 'Haldi (turmeric) and 'kumkum' (red powder and scented water) marks are put.

Bhairab Lakshmi: Observed on Tuesdays for wish fulfillment. Any framed picture of any deity must be worshipped for at least 16 Tuesdays. The ritual is widely performed these days.

One the eighth day of Durga Puja, nine unmarried girls are worshipped at many places in Madhya Pradesh. Particular days of the week are also considered auspicious and worshipped.

Himachal Pradesh

The hilly state of Himachal also performs rituals throughout the year. Some of these are:

Chaitra: Gouri Tritiya, Mahashtami, Chaitri Amabasya, Ramnavami.

Baisakh: Akhateej, Barutuni Ekadasi, Krishna Ekadasi, Ashamai, Mohini Ekadasi.

Jaistha: Barsait Amabasya, Nirjala Ekadasi, Achala Ekadasi.

Asadh: Vyas Purnima, Harisayani Ekadasi, Devasani Ekadasi, Kokila.

Sravan: Raksha Mangal, Kajari Purnima, Sravan Shukla Teej, Mangalagouri, Nagpanchami, Putrada Ekadasi.

Bhadra: Magha, Halsasthi, Janmashtami, Aja Ekadasi, Doas, Heritalika Teej, Ganesha Chaturthi, Surya Sasthi, Radhashtami, Vindayak, Uma-Maheswara *brata*, Santan Navami.

Asvin: Papankushi, Ekadasi, Ashabhagavati, Padmanava Ekadasi, Upangalalita, Dusshera.

Aghrayan: Utpanna Ekadasi, Dhana Brata, Mokshada Ekadasi.

Poush: Makar Sankranti, Chiriamuthi, Pati Brata, Bhagwan Pat, Jethan Pat.

Magh: Mouni Amabasya, Sakath Chouth, Vasant Panchami, Chowth, Ganesha Chaturthi, Shattila Ekadasi.

Falgun: Sivaratri, Janki, Ashmata, Vijaya Ekadasi, Amlaki Ekadasi, Sitala Ashtami, Holika Dahan.

Kokila Brata: Observed from the full moon night of the month of *Asadh* to keep away widowhood. It is observed when *Asadh* has an extra day which happens once in about 20 years. Kokila means the cuckoo, the bird to which Siva's wife Sati had been transformed for being instrumental in her husband spoiling her father Daksha's *yagna* (rites) for a son. Sati got back her former form after a thousand years and was remarried to Siva (myth). Mythology also has it that Daksha's head had been severed in battle and replaced with that of a goat.

The ritual also has its base in astronomy. The first sign of the zodiac was Aries (the goat's head of Daksha), then Taurus (Siva's attendant Nandi), the third Gemini or Siva-Parvati, Cancer or Ganesha with the elephant's head, Leo the lion carrier of Sati and Virgo or Sati herself.

The cuckoo resembles the crow or Corvus which lies below Virgo and so Kokila or Sati has been given precedence over the crow. The fall of Sati can also be related to the decline of Virgo in the astronomical cycle.

Rajasthan

Rajasthan always had a vast nomadic population whose roaming around helped create a unique folk culture and the emergence of regional deities out of the tales they carried for generations. Some of the rituals of Rajasthan are:

Chaitra: Dhulandi, Gangour, Sitala Ashtami, Ghudla, Navratri, Hanuman Jayanti.

Baisakh: Akhateej.

Jaistha: Nirjala Ekadasi, Dusshera, Bata Savitri.

Asadh: Guru Purnima.

Sravan: Raksha Bandhan, Teej (minor), Nagpanchami.

Bhadra: Janmashtami, Anant Chaturdasi, Ganesh Chaturthi, Teej (major), Rishi Panchami.

Asvin: Dusshera, Navratri, Dhanteras.

Kartick: Bhaiya Duj, Gopashtami, Diwali, Gowardhan, Karwa Chouth.

Aghrayan: Gita Jayanti.

Magh: Makar Sankranti, Vasant Panchami, Sivaratri, Chouth, Suraj Saptami.

Falgun: Holi.

Gangour: Symbolises the marriage of Gan (Siva) with Gour (Gouri or Parvati). The number of participants at the ritual must be uneven and no widow can take part in it. The unmarried girls pray for husbands of their choice and the married for good health of their husbands.

Punjab

The land of five rivers and it was from here that the Indo-Aryan people were believed to have spread to the whole world. Divided in 1947 with the western part going to Pakistan. Agriculture still remains a major occupation and some of the rituals are:

Chaitra: Jarga, Aan Nawan, Karna.

Baisakh: Baisakh Sankranti

Jaistha: Nirjala Ekadasi.

Asadh: Nauratan.

Sravan: Tian.

Bhadra: Gugga Naumi, Janmashtami.

Asvin: Debotthan, Dusshera.

Kartick: Diwali, Karwa Chouth, Tikka.

Poush: Lohri.

Magh: Makar Sankranti.

Falgun: Roshni, Holi.

Nirjala Ekadasi: Known in Punjab as Nimanikanti. Hindu women of Punjab fast the whole day and apply sandalwood paste to their bodies. During the period of fast not even water can be taken.

Tian: Observed in *Sravan* to herald the monsoon. Women apply henna to their hands and feet, sing and dance and newly wed ones wait for relatives and escort them to their parents' place. Sweet are made of kheer (dried milk) and offer these with songs.

Gugga Noumi: Observed in *Bhadra* to honour Gugga Pir whose portrait is painted along with a snake. Followers of the Pir go round collecting alms, carrying a decorated stick with a coconut attached at the end which is called 'Pir Danda'. Songs are sung to the Pir so that he takes care of everybody

Karwa Chouth: Ritual performed in *Kartick* for the welfare of husbands and would be husbands.

Tikka: On the day after Diwali, sisters put rice-paste 'jafran' (kind of spice) marks on their brothers' foreheads so that no evil can touch them.

Gujarat

The Hindu dominated state in Western India, Gujarat is known as much for its industry as folk art and culture. A special feature of life in the state is that while widows do observe rituals with unmarried and married women they do not have any rituals of their own. Some of the rituals of Gujarat.

Baivab Lakshmi: A Friday ritual for prosperity, it is observed by married women or unmarried girls or by men if no females are available. It has to be observed for eleven or twenty one Fridays.

Jaya-Parvati Brata: Observed on the eleventh to fifteenth day of the bright fortnight of *Asadh* for five years. While performing the ritual only one meal a day is allowed. No salt is allowed. Observed by unmarried girls for getting husbands of their choice.

Sitala Saptami: Comparable to *Sitala Sasthi* and performed for the children's welfare. Women have to eat food cooked the night before. Observed on the day before Janmastami, the birth celebration of Krishna.

Sankar or Siva Brata: Observed on the four Mondays of *Sravana* when one-fourth of a portion of *michhri* (sugarcandy) is mixed with water and taken. Performed for welfare of husbands and children and for getting good husbands.

Lakshmi Brata: Observed two days before Diwali in *Kartick* for peace and prosperity.

Navratri: Worship of the deity *Ambika* who rides a tiger. It continues for nine days in *Asvin* and men also participate. The women dance the 'garba' and a woman goes round with a clay pot ridden with holes inside which a lamp burns. The pot is the symbol of Sun and the ritual is akin to the Durga Puja of West Bengal.

Jai Santoshimata: Fried chick-peas and molasses are a must as anything sour is taboo. The women have to hold the peas and molasses while listening to the tales of the deity. Later an uneven number of boys have to be fed.

Maharashtra

The main festival is *Ganesha Chaturthi.* There are various other rituals performed in the state as also folk customs. One has a couple roaming around with idols on their heads and the man periodically beating himself with whip made of strong threads when the woman plays a musical instrument like the tambourine. In another a man moves around with a decorated bull, the animal nodding when questions are put to it.

Haldi Kumkum: Observed in almost every house to avoid the life of a widow. It is performed throughout the month of *Shravana.*

Dhanteras: Observed by women on the day before Kali Puja. Gifts of utensils are made to married women.

Ganesha Chaturthi: Observed on the fourth day of the bright fortnight every month by married women. In addition the Ganpati Puja takes place a month before Durga Puja. The song that is sung reads like, "Ganesh Baba Mareswar (another name of Ganesha), Please come early next year".

Gudi Padva: This marks the beginning of the new year on the 31st day of *Chaitra.* Women make all kinds of sweets which are distributed. Women also observe the *Bata Savitri Brata* for the health of their husbands.

Tamil Nadu

The southern state of Tamil Nadu can also be called a state of temples and the woman are known for their religiosity. Some popular rituals are:

Barlakshmi: Observed by married women on the full moon night of Shravana. The floor is decorated with alpana painting and in the centre a brass or silver pot is placed on which a coconut is kept. A painting of Lakshmi is kept as also two banana saplings.

The women fast and after their bath make five types of food with rice and pulses as also sweets which are offered to the deity. Coconuts and 'payesh' (rice pudding) are a must.

Sankranti Brata: Observed on the last day of *Poush* for the welfare of brothers.

Many other rituals are observed like *Ganesh Chaturthi. Shivaratri, Savitri Brata, Haldi Kumkum, Pongal* etc. The new year celebration is called *Onam.*

Onam is also celebrated in Andhra Pradesh as also the *Haldi Kumkum.* The later is performed in Karnataka also where the new year celebration is known as Ugadi.

Kerala

The state is known for its high rate of literacy as well as the people's aesthetic sense, as shown in the Kathakali dance in which the men performers remain silent. The new year celebration is known as Vishu.

Aiappa: A ritual performed essentially by men for a month when they sleep on blankets and do not shave or have haircuts. During this month they cook their own food and visit temples wearing black dresses. The deity being unmarried only men

and chaste women can go to the temple. The ritual is an expression of sacrifice, restraint and devotion.

Bangladesh

Before the partition of India in 1947, the same rituals were more or less observed in West and East Bengal which in 1971 emerged as Bangladesh. Rituals are still observed by the Hindus there as well as some Muslims and some of the typically East Bengal *bratas* were brought over to West Bengal by those Hindus who left their homes.

Bangladesh is at present divided into 64 districts. Some of the rituals observed in different districts:

Jessore (Magura): Akshay Ghat Brata, Falgacchano Brata, Talnabami Brata, Subachani Brata, Dakshinroy, different types of Sasthi Brata, Lakshmi Brata, Mangalchandi Brata, Savitri Brata.

Kishoreganj: Mangalchandi, Bipattarini, Santoshi Mata, Subachani, Manasa, Lakshmi, Baidyanath, Sani, Kartick, Ambubachi, Sitala, Kalkinarayan, Garasi, Aranya Sasthi or Jamai Sasthi, Kshetra Brata, Maghi Brata, Chaitra Sankranti, Bishnu Puja or Halkhata, Sumati, Bastu Puja, Sivaratri, Satyanarayan, Shrabani, Banadurga, Janmashtami, Mahalaya, Kamakshya, Surya Brata, Ghatkali Brata, Siddheswari Brata, Kanubhai Brata.

Also some Muslim rituals like Hajir Pir Brata, Khwaj Pir Brata, and joint Hindu-Muslim rituals like Asan Pir Brata, Kanu Pir Brata and Gawa Pir Brata.

Chittagong: Satya Pir, Manik Pir, Dalan Pir, Mangal Chandi, Sankat Chandi, Jaimangal Chandi, Surya Brata, Asvinikumar, Sitala Brata, Lakshmi Purnima, Dhanya, Purnima,

Katyani, Kartikeya, Joylakumari, Maghadeswari, Andeshwari Brata, Buraburi, Irhawali, Subachani, Anant Chaturdasi, Talnavami, Lalita Saptami, Belbhata, Jamai Sasthi, Bhai Phonta.

Sylhet: Bratas, month-wise:

Baisakh: Akshay Tritia (third day of full moon), Harishmangal Chandi (Tuesday), Sankata Brata (Friday).

Jaistha: Aranya Sasthi sixth day of the bright fortnight), Savitri Brata from the 13th day of the dark fortnight to the new moon.

Asadh: Ambubachi from the seventh day for three days.

Sravan: Nagpanchami on the fifth day of the dark fortnight, Bishari on the last day of the month and Sankata on Fridays.

Bhadra: Ananta Brata on the fifth day of the bright fortnight, Durbashtami and Radhashtami on the eighth day, Janmashtami and on the last day Bhadra Chandi.

Asvin: Birashtami on the eighth day of Durga Puja, Lakshmi Brata, Bhratri Dwitiya on the second day of the bright fortnight, Aat Anaj on the last day.

Kartick: Ghostashtami on the eighth day of the bright fortnight, Kartick Brata on the last day and Sankata Brata on Fridays.

Aghrayan: Nabanna Parban Brata and on any Tuesday Kulkar Mangalchandi Brata.

Poush: Poush Parban on the last day.

Magh: Magh Brata, Sital Sasthi, on the eighth day of the bright fortnight, Sri Panchami Brata, Surya Brata, on any Sunday, Sankata on Fridays.

Chaitra: Ramnavami on the ninth day of the bright fortnight, Siva Brata on the last day by Gajan Sanyasis, those who worship Shiva.

The Rituals of Shaka and Faridpur that deserve mention are, Jal Sankranti, Lalita, Ananta which are observed by both married women and widows. Some are the exclusive preserves of married woman, like, Savitri, Akshay Sindoor, Dadhi Sankranti e(y)o Sankranti. Many other rituals are also observed like Jamai Sasthi, Bhratri Dwitia, Nistarini, Nirakali, Satyanarayn, Ghatkali, Tara, Satya Pir, Parameswari, Manikpir, Mushkil Asan, Kshtera, Punyi Pukur, Gorakshanath, Kojagari Lakshmi, Alakshmi, Banbibi, Garasi, Mangal Chandi, Janmashtami, Bipattarini, Gawa Pir, Hajir Pir, Khawaj Khijir.

Fifty one Bratas observed in Bangladesh:

1. *Chhay Sasthi:* Continuously for six days in the room where a baby is born.

2. *Rathai Chandi:* On the day of the Rath or Chariot Festival in Asadh.

3. *Garai Brata:* On the last day of Asvin.

4. *Basanta Brata:* Saturdays and Tuesdays of Chaitra.

5. *Jamai Sasthi Aranya Sasthi:* Month of Jaistha according to almanac.

6. *Karmadi Brata:* Last day of Jaistha.

7. *Kshetra Brata :* Observed in Aghrayan with freshly harvested rice.

8. *Maghi Purnima:* On full moon of *Magh.*

9. *Chaitra Sankranti:* Last day of *Chaitra.*

10. *Vishnu Puja or Halkhata:* Bengali new year's day.
11. *Nabanna:* With new rice in *Aghrayan.*
12. *Sumati Brata:* On any Monday or Friday.
13. *Kalkinarayan:* On any Saturday or Tuesday.
14. *Santoshi Mata:* On 16 Fridays as pledged.
15. *Jwarajwuri Brata:* To get cured of illness.
16. *Haji Pir Brata:* Performed by Muslim women to get back lost things.
17. *Mangal Chandi:* On any Tuesday.
18. *Bipadnashini Brata:* On any Saturday or Tuesday.
19. *Bastu Puja:* During *Poush Parvana* on the last day of Poush.
20. *Sivaratri:* In *Chaitra.*
21. *Satyanarayan/Sani:* On Saturdays of the dark fortnight or in *Baisakh, Asadh, Magh* according to the almanac.
22. *Sravani Brata:* On the last day of *Shravan.*
23. *Bandurga:* To mark the end of the impure period after a person's death or before a happy occasion like marriage.
24. *Janmashtami:* Observed in *Bhadra.*
25. *Analaya:* Observed under a neem tree to pray for the peace of departed souls.
26. *Niyam Seva Brata:* Observed by Vaishnavites either from mid *Asvin* to mid *Kartick* or the whole of *Kartick.*

27. *Subachani Brata:* On Saturdays and Tuesdays.

28. *Kartick Puja:* On the last day of *Kartick.*

29. *Kamakshya :* On Saturdays and Tuesdays.

30. *Surya Brata:* In *Aghrayan* with newly harvested rice.

31. *Barkumar Brata:* Prior to any happy event.

32. *Ghatkali Brata:* On Saturday and Tuesday.

33. *Aleri Brata:* On any Friday night in *Bhadras.*

34. *Siddheswari Brata:* Sundays or Thursdays of the bright fortnight of *Bhadra.*

35. *Asan Pir Brata:* Saturday and Tuesday (Kishoreganj and Noakhali districts).

36. *Kanu Bhai Brata:* Sundays and Thursdays of *Bhadra* to bring good fortune.

37. *Baidyanath:* Observed on Mondays.

38. *Sankattarini Brata:* Observed on Tuesday, Thursday, Saturday and Sunday.

39. *Gorakhanath Seca:* On the last day of *Chaitra.*

40. *Panchkumar Brata:* On the last day of *Chaitra* and the first day of *Kartick.*

41. *Rupasi Brata:* For the children's welfare.

42. *Madar Banser Jari Brata:* For protection against fire.

43. *Kaua or Kak Brata:* For protecting crops from birds and animals—*kak* is the crow.

44. *Basanta Brata:* As protection from *basanta* or small-pox.

45. *Yatali brata:* To be cured of skin diseases.

46. *Jhalka Brata:* To keep away *Laotha* or cholera.

47. *Mathmandal Brata:* Addressed to the Sun.

48. *Hanchra Brata:* Observed on the first day of *Poush.*

49. *Bagnai Brata:* To keep away tigers.

50. *Poush Aglano Brata:* Observed on the last day of *Poush.*

In some of these rituals the women perform the Dhamail dance, some are associated with the fertility theme and powers of the supernatural like the *Surya Brata.* In some the forms of prayers in ancient societies can be noticed like the *Nagh Mandal Brata.* Tree worship is noticed in *Rupasi Brata.*

Dr Ashraf Siddiqui has pointed out, the ritual or the *brata* had its origin in pre-Hindu, pre-Buddhist days and was influenced by later developments such as the mixing of Aryans and non-Aryans. Buddhism also influenced the rituals.

From the very birth a person is brought up on rituals and their tales. The new mother listens carefully to such tales in the hope that the child will benefit from the fact that these are being told. Similarly rituals are observed for welfare which is the positive side of the *brata.* The negative side is the superstition that these help to ward off evil spirits.

Muslims as a rule do not observe such rituals but those converted to the faith do and they comprise about five per cent of the community. They have also started painting the alpana, of course more for decoration than anything else. Dr Momen Chowdhury says there is no such thing as a Muslim ritual but these are observed if the same purpose is to be achieved.

Dr Wakil Ahmed sees these rituals as lively elements of folklore. Not only do these have regional peculiarities, the tales also vary from the time of the first narration to later days, incorporating noticable changes. History can be traced through some of the rhymes of the rituals, particularly those related to trade and commerce.

Following his field surveys, Mohammad Saidur has noticed the prevalence of such rituals among the lower caste Hindus. He says only the *Khawaj Pir* is a Muslim ritual and restricted to those who practice the Ayurvedic system of medicine. He has also analysed the place of numbers in the rituals:

One is the symbol of the Supreme Being or Brahma.
Two is the symbol of eyes (two).

Three symbolises the Trinity-Brahma, Vishnu, Maheswar and also indicates Agni or Fire.

Five, the five chaste women or Panchakanya (Ahalya, Draupadi, Kunti, Tara, Mandodari) as also the five Pandavas, Yudhisthira, Bhima, Arjun, Nakul and Sahadev.

Seven—the Sea.

The Manasa ritual is still performed in Kishoreganj villages and there are artists specialising in the painting on spongewood which are needed for the ritual. A fair is held in connection with the *brata* at which only things needed for its observance are sold.

Let us take a closer look at some of the common rituals observed in Bangladesh.

Panchkumar Brata: Observed on the last day of Chaitra by expecting women who, after bathing in the morning, arrange on a banana leaf 'khoi' (parched rice), chura (flattened rice), chhatu (maize or barley flour), bananas, sugar, flowers etc. This is the offering to the deity who has no idol. After the ceremony the offering is taken out and the ritual is considered a success if a crow eats it.

The story of the ritual is about the unmarried daughter of a Brahmin who had unwittingly swallowed the semen of Mahadeva and in the given birth to five sons (Panch Kumar). When they grew up they found nobody was willing to mix with them as they did not know who their father was. They asked their mother who told them to find out from Mahadev who came to the river to bathe every day. He told them they were his sons.

The five sons acquired supernatural powers and people came to rever them and the ritual of worshipping them was established. They are supposed to bring peace and prosperity.

Chilai Brata: Observed generally by the weaving community. Implements needed in the profession are collected with great care and the alpana painting includes the picture of a 'cheel' bird or the kite. After the ritual, she narrates the story which runs as follows:

There was a king who had six daughters and no sons. When his queen was expecting again, he decided that if another daughter was born he would kill the queen. Unfortunately, it was a daughter again but the women in the palace did not tell the king that. They said a dead child had been delivered, put the new born babe in a clay pot and left it in the sea.

As the pot floated away a kite noticed it and finding the baby decided to bring it up as his own. Twelve years passed when the son of a merchant discovered and married her with the permission of the kite. The bird gave one of her feathers to the daughter at the time of departure and said if she was in trouble she would just have to hold it to the fire and she would arrive.

The merchant's son had six brothers and their wives got jealous of their sister-in-law. They were all weavers and asked the new bride to make clothes for the new year. She did as the kite had said and her problem was solved. From that day began the ritual of Chilai or Worship of the Kite.

Biskaram Brata: Observed by weavers and potters on the first day of *Baisakh.* Here also the story is the same of how a kite came to the rescue of the youngest daughter-in-law and how the bird came to be revered from that day.

Āt Anāj Brata: Common in Sylhet. A preparation of right vegetables (*Āt Anāj*) is made and distributed on the last day of *Asvin* and first day of *Kartick* by married women. The ritual is addressed to Lakshmi for prosperity.

Subachani Brata: Observed after marriages to wish the newly wed couple well.

The ritual is performed on Saturdays or Tuesdays and the ingredients include rice-paste, vermillion, oil, turmeric, sessame, wood-apple (bel) leaves, honey, sugar, clarified butter, betel-leaves, betel-nuts, sari etc. The alpana has motifs of twin ducks. Married women stand in a row and the 'brati' washes their feet and dries them with her sari end which is wiped on the newly married girl's head.

Basanda Brata: Observed to keep away small-pox. Banana trees numbering the same as the number of people in the house are tied together and an equal number of dolls are made with grounded rice. These are placed on banana leaves before a pitcher and *chura, khoi, chhatu,* molasses, bananas, milk, clarified butter, honey placed on other banana leaves and eaten by the women after the priest completes the ritual. Rice is forbidden on the occasion.

Basanda is the elder sister of Sitala who also is worshipped for keeping the same disease away. The ritual is performed in the month of *Chaitra.*

Aleri Brata: On a Friday in *Bhadra* three types of pies are made, one with dried fish stuffing, one without salt and one with salt. Performed by married women at night to drive away misfortune. There are no rules and everything can be eaten.

Siddheswari Brata: Observed in the bright fortnight of *Bhadra* on Sundays or Thursdays, in the night. Pies without salt and with salt are needed. Purpose again is to drive away misfortune.

Asan Pir Brata: Observed on Saturdays or Tuesdays for the safe return home of those away on work. A wooden seat is covered with a decorated cloth (ason) and offerings of rice and nine types of edible creepers (*shāāk*) are made along with lemon leaves. The woman whose husband is away has to eat the whole amount and nothing else. Observed by both Hindus and Muslims.

Ghātkali Brata: To appease the deity Kali who resides on the banks of rivers and ponds-ghat. Performed next to a water body but where none exists, a stone tray is filled with water, kept in front of a basil tree and the ritual observed to keep dangers away.

Kalkinarayan Brata: A male ritual which involves smoking from the bowl of a hookah by seven men.

Kamakshya Brata: For wish fulfillment. No rules except that the *brati* must fast and pray to the deity Kamaksha. She breaks her fast in the evening with grounded rice.

Surya Brata: A tribute to Lakshmi but named Surya or Sun because it is performed in sunlight. Observed on Thursdays or Sundays after the new crop is harvested. Offerings are made of grounded rice, molasses, milk, clarified butter, honey and bananas.

Madar Banser Jari: Madar is the Pir who fights fire. Two types of bamboos (*bansh*) are needed, one of which must have marks resembling eyes or nose. One is taken as the symbol of Madar Pir and the other of Khawaj Khijir. The ritual is observed in the month of *Magh* when fires break out. Those observing it collect rice from the villagers to make *shirni*, a type of sweet, which is distributed among all. The ritual takes on a festival look and fair are held on the occasion.

Rituals invoking rain: During spells of drought, young men of the village collect broken rice and pulses and with the help of girls make a kind of gruel at a central spot which is distributed. Then the girls make a hole which is filled with water and two frogs are married—frogs are believed to herald rain.

Professor Wakil Ahmed has spoken of many such rituals, including *Megha Rani, Basudhara, Punyi Pukur. Megha Rani* (Queen of Cloud) is observed by the Muslims while *Punyi Pukur* is a Hindu ritual. The Rajbanshis of Rangpur-Jalpaiguri also have their own rituals for the purpose.

Belbhata or Kalkumar Brata: Prevalent in the Anwara region of Chittagong and observed through Baisakh for wealth and male children. On any Sunday morning the woman performing the ritual sits down to eat with relatives after offering some rice, vegetables cooked in *ghee* (clarified butter) and two chinarose garlands which are left by a pond. After sunset no cereals can be eaten.

The ritual has a long song celebrating the glory of different deities and the way they come to the aid of mankind.

Nepal

The world's only Hindu kingdom, Nepal for the most part is a land of extreme poverty and the Nepalese have to undergo tremendous hardship to eke out a living. This hardship is manifest in their rituals which involve fasting and staying awake at nights. Some of these are:

Sri Ram Navami Brata: Observed in the ninth day of the bright fortnight of *Chaitra*. The person observing it has to fast the whole day, listen to the epic Ramayana and write the name of Rama ten thousand times on paper, sleep on the barren floor at night. The next day the place of the ritual is bounded off with banana trees, decorated with flowers and conch shells and a picture of Hanuman, the disciple of Rama. Then is worshipped through one hundred and eight offering of clarified butter to Agni or fire. Gifts are distributed among the Brahmins. It is believed that the ritual opens the gates of heaven.

Sri Krishnashtami Brata: Observed in the last week of *Shravan* when Krishna is worshipped in a decorated pandal. The *brati* has to fast the whole day and stay awake with others in the night when there is dancing and singing of songs.

According to mythology, pleased with the prayers of Devaki and Basudeva, Vishnu got born as their son Krishna. It is believed that the ritual leads to such sons being born to those who perform it.

Haritalika Brata: Performed on the third day of the bright fortnight of *Bhadra*. The ways of the ritual were supposed to have been taught to Parvati by her husband Lord Shiva.

Idols of Shiva and Parvati are made with sand and installed at the centre of a pandal and donation of rice, fruits, coconuts and betel-nuts are made, on the day after the ritual. On the actual day the *brati* fasts and listens to tales of Mahadeva and Haritalika. The next day food and clothes are distributed among the poor. The ritual is for a happy married life and good husbands for unmarried girls.

Kojagar Lakshmi Brata: Observed in *Asvin*. The *brati* has to fast the whole day and decorate the house with a maximum of one hundred thousand and a minimum of hundred lamps. Then the deity Lakshmi is installed, worshipped and the night spent in games of cards or dice. The next morning Indra is worshipped and gifts of food and money given to Brahmins. The ritual is for long life and heavenly abode for the soul after death. Also health and wealth in this world.

Picture of Ahoi Asthami.

12

Brata : Comparisons

The story of Savitri is the story of great devotion to her husband Satyaban which ultimately persuaded even Yama to return him to life and grant her other wishes for her near and dear ones. In Maharashtra and the Hindu speaking belt the ritual is known as *Bata Savitri Brata.* As the chart shows there are a few variations in the manner in which the ritual is observed but the purpose remains the same, namely the husbands welfare. [Table 1]

The ritual is observed but again with some differences in the manner of observance between Bengali women and those in other places. Everybody, however, is of the opinion that the Earth should not be disturbed during the three days and that she is an impure state as society believed women to be in those days of the month. [Table 2]

An essentially widows' ritual among Bengalis, to highlight their spirit of renunciation and discipline, is one seen as an occasion to keep fit by men and women in other states. The Mahabharata has Kunti shivering in cold after bathing for *ekadasi* in the month of *Magh*, seeing which Bhima removed the cold. This, however, annoyed Varuna who wanted Krishna's intervention—Varuna is the deity of water and Bhima had cooled an iron rod in a pond. Krishna ordained that Varuna will not have to suffer the heat if Bhima also observes the ritual which he did and this ritual came to be known as *Bhaimi Ekadasi.* [Table 3]

The name *Karticksnan* has come from the practice of bathing early in the morning in a river or a pond. Only in Orissa do the women have to follow restrictions in matter of food. Also only in West Bengal and Bangladesh is it observed for handsome male children and in other states for general welfare. [Table 4]

The differences in the observance of *Jitashtami* are not to be found only in different states but within West Bengal also. For instance, the mention of vulture and she-fox is to be found only in the narration of the ritual in Bankura and Bishnupur. The story of the *brata* is how king Salibahan observed Jitashtami and got a son and a daughter. The son was named *Jimatbahan* whose children all died after birth till the observance of Jitashtami brought a son who lived. [Table 5]

There are two tales relating to the ritual in the Hindu belt. One is about how king Jimutbahan saved snakes from the greed of Garuda. The other is the story of the Mahabharata of how Krishna had saved Parikshit while he was still in the womb of Uttara (Arjuna's daughter-in-law) from the wrath of Ashvathama. The ritual is named Jeotia after the manner in which Parikshit's life was saved (Jeo-Live).

In Bihar the women arrange fruits on a wooden tray, cover it and bathe it. There is no such custom in Uttar Pradesh.

The *Santoshi Mata Brata* seems to have travelled to Bangladesh from West Bengal. The tale is of a women Savitri whose husband Ramla had gone elsewhere to work and she was being tortured by the wives of his brothers. One day she heard of Santoshi Ma, worshipped her on Fridays and Ramlal came back and they became rich. However, goaded by her jealous sisters-in-law, their children took money from her and ate sour condiments. This annoyed the deity and the family once again became poor. Savitri, however, continued worshipping the deity and ultimately she was appeased and they got back everything and even sons were born to her. [Table 6]

An interesting thing about the ritual is that it is observed more in urban areas than in villages.

Picture of Brata, Bihar.

Table 1 : Savitri Brata

W. Bengal/ Bangladesh	*Orissa*	*Tamil Nadu*	*Maharashtra*	*Bihar, UP, MP, Rajasthan*
Savitri Chaturdasi	Savitri Amabasya	Savitri	Bata Savitri	Bata Savitri
Dark fortnight of Jaistha-14th day	On new moon of Jaistha	Last day of *Magh*	On new moon of *Magh*	Same as Orissa
Bratini Bathes and wears purified clothes	Bathes and wears new clothes	Wears weeding sari	Wears purified clothes	Same as Maharashtra
For husband's welfare	Same	Same	Same	Same
Married women perform	Same	Same	Same	Same
No amulet	Same	Yellow amulet	No amulet	No amulet
Observed at home	Same	Same	Same	Same
String wound round bamboo pole	No such rule	No such rule	String tied round banyan branch	String tied round banyan branch
Brahmins and married women fed	All are fed	Couple eats rice ball and molasses	All are fed	All are fed

(Contd.)

(Table Contd.)

W. Bengal/ Bangladesh	*Orissa*	*Tamil Nadu*	*Maharashtra*	*Bihar, UP, MP, Rajasthan*
Vermillion and lac-dye given to married women	No system	No system	Married women put haldi and Kumkum marks on each other	Vermillion given to married women
Husband's feet are touched as mark of respect	Same	Same	Same	Same
Ritual has a tale to be narrated	Same	No tale	No tale	Has a tale to be narrated

Table 2 : Ambubachi Brata

	W. Bengal/Bangladesh	*Assam*	*Orissa*	*MP, UP, Rajasthan*	*Nepal*
1.	Ambubachi	Amti	Rajasankranti	Rishipanchami	Rishipanchami
2.	Widows perform	Widows and menstruating women	Unmarried girls	Women and Men	All Women
3.	Three days from Asadh 7	Three days from Asadh	Last 2 days of Jaistha, Asaṛh	Fifth day of bright fortnight in *Bhadra*	Same as MP, for four days
4.	Not dedicated to anybody	Not dedicated	Not dedicated	For Saptamuni	Saptamuni
5.	Nothing cooked eaten	Nothing cooked eaten	Nothing cooked eaten	No bar	No bar
6.	Fruits, sago eaten	Fruits, fresh milk taken	Watered rice, sweet during day, nothing at night	No rules	Vegetables, wild fruits in evening
7.	No physical labour	Same	Same	Same	Same

(Contd.)

(Table Contd.)

	W. Bengal/Bangladesh	*Assam*	*Orissa*	*MP, UP, Rajasthan*	*Nepal*
8.	Not to touch anything	Same	Same	Same	Same
9.	No Puja allowed	Same	Earth worship after 3 days	Puja with various ingredients	Saptamuni Puja
10.	Earth believed to menstruate	Same	Same	No mention	No mention
11.	No farming allowed	Same	Same	No mention	No mention
12.	Generally rains	Rains heavily	Rain plays no part	Rain plays no part	Rain plays no part
13.	Bratini bathes after 3 days	Bratini bathes after 3 days	On all days, 1st and 2nd with turmeric	Bathes and wears clean clothes	First day only with water then with sesame and amlaki (myrobalan).

(Contd.)

(Table Contd.)

	W. Bengal/Bangladesh	*Assam*	*Orissa*	*MP, UP, Rajasthan*	*Nepal*
14.	Believed milk in room keeps snakes away	Same belief	Nothing mentioned	Nothing	Nothing
15.	No tales	No tales	No tales	Tale indicating significance	Same
16.	No result indicated but observance a must	A must and farmers expect bumper crops	A Must	Ritual brings peace and prosperity	Ritual brings peace and prosperity

Table 3 : Ekadasi Brata

W. Bengal/Bangladesh	*Orissa*	*Bihar*	*MP, UP, Rajasthan*
1. Ekadasi	Same	Same	Same
2. Many types of Ekadasi	Same	Same	Same
3. Observed every month	Same	Same	Same
4. Widows perform and men in some cases	Married women perform only if husbands also do so.	Men and married women perform in *Kartick*	Married women perform only if husbands do.
5. Restrictions on manner of observance	Same	Same	Same—No menstruating women allowed to perform
6. No rice products eaten	No rice, wheat products allowed	No rice, bread, salt, mustard oil on day of ritual	No rice allowed.
7. Rules more important than actual puja	Rules more important	Puja in morning after bath	Observing rule more important
8. Observed to keep body fit	Same	Same	Same
9. Bhaimi Ekadasi ritual has a tale	No tale	No tale	Tales in some cases

Table 4 : Kartick Sankranti or Kartick Purnima Brata

W. Bengal/Bangladesh	*Orissa*	*Tamil Nadu*	*Bihar, U.P., Rajasthan*
1. Known as Kartick Sankranti or Kartick Brata	Karticksnan	Kartick Purnima	Kartick Purnima or Karticksnan
2. Married women perform	All women also men	All women	All women
3. On last day of Kartick	Full moon in Kartick	Full moon in Kartick	Full moon in Kartick
4. Kartick deity worshipped	Radha-Krishna ritual	Puja performed	Puja performed
5. For male child	For general welfare	For general welfare	For general welfare
6. Fasting is a must	Same	Same	Same
7. No system of bathing in river	Must bathe in river	No such system	Must bathe in river or pond

(Contd.)

(Table Contd.)

W. Bengal/Bangladesh	Orissa	Tamil Nadu	Bihar, U.P., Rajasthan
8. Observed one day	For fortnight or month	One day	One day
9. Eat only once on the ritual day	Eat boiled sunned rice and ghee	No such system	No such system
10. Can't eat while eating nor sleep during the day	No restrictions	No restrictions	No restrictions
11. Odderings distributed only among children	Distributed among all	Distributed among all	Distributed among all
12. Pitchers painted with alpana design to become 'Brata Bhanda' of vessels of the ritual. Collyrium is made from a lamp in the pitcher and applied to children's eyes for their long life.	Sand and clay used to make a temple like structure on river banks and these are decorated.	No such system	No such system

Table 5 : Jitashtami Brata

W.Bengal/Bangladesh	*Orissa*	*Bihar, UP, Rajasthan, MP*
1. Jitashtami	Jitashtami	Jiwatputtika or Jeotia
2. Observed on eighth day of Dark fortnight if Asvin	Fifteen days after Radhashtami in Bhadra	Eighth day of dark fortnight of *Asvin*
3. Mainly by married women sometimes also by husbands	By married women	By married women
4. Have to fast whole day	Same	Same
5. Have to create pond by digging hole and filling it with water	No such system	No such system
6. Peas have to be soaked	Peas have to be soaked	Kalai (leguminous seed) has to be soaked
7. Observed at home	Same	Same
8. No food restriction	No food restriction	Food can't be chewn, must be swallowed straight

(Contd.)

(Table Contd.)

	W. Bengal/Bangladesh	*Orissa*	*Bihar, UP, Rajasthan, MP*
9.	A pitcher is decorated	No such system	No such system
10.	Children participate	No	No
11.	Amulets not needed but coloured threads tied round children's throats	Amulets needed	Amulets of red, yellow threads worn
12.	Brati must bathe in pond or river	No rules about bathing	Have to bathe in pond or river
13.	Offerings distributed	Same	Same
14.	Tale has reference of vulture but not kite	No reference to either vulture or kite	Tale talks of kite but not vulture.
15.	Images of vulture, she-fox made	No images made	No images made
16.	Brati prays for children and their well being	Same	Same
17.	Jimutbahan mentioned	Same	Same
18.	System of listening to the narration	Same	Same

Table 6 : Santoshimata Brata

	W. Bengal/Bengladesh	*Orissa*	*Bihar*	*UP, MP, Gujarat South India*	*Nepal*
1.	Santoshimata Brata	Same	Same	Same	Same
2.	Observed on Friday	Same	Same	Same	Same
3.	Unmarried and married women perform	Same	All women	All women	All women
4.	Pitcher of deity ceremoniously placed	Same	Same	Same	No system
5.	Women have to fast	Same	Same	No mention of fasting	Have to fast
6.	Observed at least 16 times	Same	Same	Same	At least 3 months
7.	Every week one more lamp is needed	Same	Same	Same	No system
8.	Restrictions on Observance	Same	Same	Same	Same

(Contd.)

(Table Contd.)

	W. Bengal/Bengladesh	*Orissa*	*Bihar*	*UP, MP, Gujarat South India*	*Nepal*
9.	Anything sour is taboo	Same	Same	Same	Same
10.	No stellar positions to be considered	Same	Same	Same	Same
11.	Peas and molasses a must	Same	Same	Same	peas and brown sugar
12.	Vegetarian food a must	Same	Same	Same	Same
13.	Rituals has a tale	Same	Same	Same	Same
14.	Tale has to be heard with peas and molasses in hand	Same	Same	Same	No such system
15.	Five or seven boys fed after ritual	Same	Same	Eight boys or Brahmins fed and given money	Eight boys below 12 fed
16.	No system of giving money	Same	Same	System exists	No system
17.	Part of offerings fed cows	Same	Same	Same	No system
18.	Observed for general well-being	Same	Same	For wish fulfilment	For wish fulfilment
19.	Wishes believed to be fulfiled	Same	Same	Same	Same

Rituals Commonly Practised in Tripura, West Bengal, Bangladesh : A Comparison

Tripura	*West Bengal*	*Bangladesh*
Magh Mandal	Observed widely	In Chittagong, Comilla, Noakhali
Baghai	Bana Durga, Dakshinroy in the Sunderbans	Offerings of rice, milk and fruits made to Bana Bibi, Olabibi, Kalu Gazi
Bhadra Chandi	Observed widely	In Sylhet
Kshetra Brata	Observed widely	Observed in most districts
Ashta Lokpal (in S-W)	No such ritual but some similarity with tale of Itu *brata*	In Comilla, Noakhali, Chandpur
Uday Mangal	Observed widely	In Sylhet, Mymensingh
Manik Pir (N-W)	Observed in 24-Parganas, Hooghly, Nadia for different reasons	In Sylhet, Mymensingh, Brahmanbaria
Khawaj Brata	Not observed	In Sylhet, Mymensingh, Brahmanbaria

(Contd.)

(Table Contd.)

Tripura	*West Bengal*	*Bangladesh*
Jhatpat Thakur	Not observed	In Kishoreganj
Samayatrani	Not observed	In Sylhet, Mymensingh, Kishoreganj, Brahmanbaria
Garai Brata	In some areas	In Sylhet, Brahmanbaria
Dhanya Purnima	Not observed	In Chittagong, Noakhali, Comilla Brahmanbaria
Bhola Pora	Not observed	Dhaka, Jessore, Sylhet, Mymensingh, Brahmanbaria
Komar	Not observed	In Sylhet, Mymensingh, Brahmanbaria
Kamhat	Not observed	In Sylhet, Brahmanbaria
Banger Biya (frog's marriage)	Kulo Namano (Bringing Down the Winnow), Banger Biya	In Sylhet
Kal Bhairab	Same as above	In Sylhet

Purpose wise : West Bengal, Bangladesh, Tripura

Purpose	*West Bengal*	*Bangladesh*	*Tripura*
Curing illness	Banberuno, Thakthaki Panchra Puja	Kanu Pir, Gawa Pir, Manik Ourm Jurjuri	Chamar Jhi, Maghini
Crops and wealth	Lakshmi, Nakhchhut Punyipukur, Basudhara Asvatha Bat, Senjuti, Harir Charan	Bhola Pora, Samayarani Lakshmi, Senjuti Harir Charan	Kalbhairb, Khawaj, Bhola Pore, Samayatrani Thanki Thakrun
More crops	Kshetra Brata	Kshetra Brata	Samayatrani
Getting back lost things	Kalkinarayan	Kalkinarayan, Haji Pir	Kshetra Brata
Family's well-being	Sivaratri, Itu Senjuti, Savitri Kulkulti	Panchkumar, Aleri, Aat Anaj	
Cattle Welfare	Soubhagya	Siddheswari	Akulonir Brata
Against tiger	Gokal, Gorakshanath Banabibi, Dakshinroy	Gokal, Gorakshanath Manik Pir, Olabibi Kalu Gazi	Manikpir, Baghai

(Contd.)

(Table Contd.)

Purpose	*West Bengal*	*Bangladesh*	*Tripura*
Surya Puja	Udaymangalchandi	Udaymangalchandi	
Against fire	Magh Mandal	Magh Mandal	Udaymangalchandi
For rain	Punyipukur, Basudhara Haat Ghurni, Kulo Namano	Kuloghat, Banger Bya	Komai
Safe return from business trip	Bhaduli	Asan Pir Brata	
Child's wellbeing	Sankata, Bipattarini	Ghatkali, Bipattarini	
To stop rain	Sasthi, Musafir	Sasthi, Rupasi,	Komai

Chart Showing Purpose of Bratas and Observance in Different States and Outside

	Purpose	*W. Bengal*	*Tripura*	*Assam*	*Orissa*
1.	Husband's Wellbeing	Different Sasthis, Sivaratri, Joymangalbar Kartickpuja, Jitashtami Bhēnpu		Sivaratri	Jitashtami Kukkuti Sivaratri
2.	Husband's wellbeing	Savitri Chauturdasi	-	-	Savitri Amabasya
3.	Family's wellbeing	Sivaratri, Senjuti Kulkulti, Itu	Bhadrachandi Dhanya Purnima	Sivaratri	Sivachauturdasi
4.	For brothers	Bhatridwitiya	-	-	Bhatridwitya
5.	General Welfare	Santoshimata, Satyanarayan, Kalkinarayan etc	Santoshimata Kalkinarayan, Jhatpatthakur	Santoshimata	Santoshimata Khudkurni Osha Makar Sankranti
6.	For Crops	Tush-Tushli, kshetra	kshetra	-	Akshay Tritia

(Contd.)

(Table Contd.)

	Purpose	W. Bengal	Tripura	Assam	Orissa
7.	Wish fulfillment Santoshi Mata, Katyani	Karam, Subachani Uday Mangal Dhanya Purnima	Santoshi Mata	Santoshi Mata	Santoshimata Kumarpurnima Budhai Osha
8.	Prosperity	Lakshmi, Bhanjo, Tushu	Thanki Thakrun Bhola Pora	Maroi	Lakshmi
9.	Related to Pir	Manikpir	-	-	
10.	Overcoming Trouble	Sankata, Bipattarini Mushkil Asan	Samaytrani	-	Ganesh Chaturthi
11.	Good Fortune Happy Married Life	Saubhagya Chaturthi Adar Simhasan Baluka, Meleni Raldurga,	-	-	-
12.	Combating Evil Forces	-	Maghini	-	-
13.	Sun Worship	Maghmandal, Lal Thakur Brata	Maghmandal, Ashta Lokapala	-	-
14.	Washing Off Sin	Ambubachi	-	Ambubachi	Shiva Chaturdasi

(Contd.)

(Table Contd.)

	Purpose	*W. Bengal*	*Tripura*	*Assam*	*Orissa*
15.	Curing Illness	Olaichandi, Panchra Puja, Ghentu, Sitala Ashoka Sasthi etc	Kamkhat, Kal Bhairab, Khawaj etc.	Maroi	Samba Dasami
16.	For rain	Punyipukur, Basudhara, Haat Ghurni, Banger Biye, Kuloghat, Hudum Chuka	Banger Biye	-	Chatua Sankranti
17.	Cow Worship	Gokaal, Manikpir, Shukh Bhanta	Manikpur	-	Bandana *brata*
18.	Keeping away Wild Animals	Bånabibi, Dakshinroy Kalugazi	Baghai	-	-
19.	Overcoming Fear of Snakes	Manasa, Nagpanchami Arandhan	-	-	Nagchowthi
20.	Attaining Heaven	Different ekadasis, Bhoot Chaturdasi	-	-	Ekadasis, Damodar

(Contd.)

(Table Contd.)

	Purpose	W. Bengal	Tripura	Assam	Orissa
21.	Day-specific	Thursday (Lakshmi) Friday (Santoshi Mata) Tuesday (Mangal Chandi) Saturday (Sani)	Same	Same	Same
22.	Stopping Rain	Musafir	-	-	-
23.	For suitable groom	Sivaratri Sanjha, Bateswara Puja	-	Sivaratri	Sivaratri
24.	Preventing Fire	-	Komai	-	-
25.	Lunar Day-specific	Purnima, Amabasya, Ekadasi Sankranti	Same	Same	Same
26.	Keeping Well	Ekadasi	-	-	Ekadasi
27.	Recovering Lost Property	Subachani, Ateswar	Dhanya Purnima	-	-
28.	Protection From Storm	Pavan Devata worship			

Chart Showing Purpose of Bratas and Observance in Different States and Outside

Bihar, M.P., U.P. Rajasthan	*Maharashtra*	*South India*	*Punjab*
Batasavitiri, Teej, Ganesha Chaturthi, Haldi Kumkum, Gangaur (Rajasthan)	Bata Savitri, Haldi Kumkum	Savitri	Karwa Chauth
Sivaratri, Chhat, Jeotia Ahoi Ashtami	-	Sivaratri	-
Sivaratri, Teej	-	-	-
Yama Dwitia	-	Kartick Purnima Sankranti Brata	Tikka Brata
Kartick Purnima Santoshi Mata, Karwar Chouth, Satyanarayan Gangaur (Rajasthan)	Santoshi Mata Guri Parwa	Santoshi Mata, Guri Parwa	-
-	-	-	-
Santoshi Mata Bhairab Lakshmi	Santoshi Mata	Santoshi Mata	-
Kojagari Lakshmi	Kojagari Lakshmi Ganesha Chaturthi	Kojagari Lakshmi Ganesha Chaturthi Barlakshmi Brata	- Gugganoumi

(Contd.)

(Table Contd.)

Bihar, M.P., U.P. Rajasthan	*Maharashtra*	*South India*	*Punjab*
Somavati Amabasya	-	-	-
Baraha Chaturdasi	-	-	-
Chhat Puja, Magh Saptami	Magha Saptami, Ratha	-	-
Surya Sasthi, Rishi Panchami (M.P.), Putra Saptami	Saptami, Putra Saptami		
Teej	-	-	Tian
Nagpanchmi	-	-	-
Narak Chaturdasi	-	Aiappa (Kerala)	Nirjala
Masoprobas			Ekadasi
Lakshmi (Thursday)	Santoshi Mata	Santoshi mata	-
Santoshi Mata (Friday)	(Friday)	(Friday)	
Sivaratri	-	Sivaratri	-
Ekadasi, Sankranti,	Sankranti, Ekadasi,	Sankranti, Purnima,	-
Purnima, Amabasya	Purnima, Amabasya	Ekadasi, Amabasya	

Chart Showing Purpose of Bratas and Observance in Different States and Outside

Gujarat	*Bangladesh*	*Nepal*
-	Savitri Chaturdasi	-
Sitala Saptami	Different Sasthis Joy Mangalbar Kartick Brata	-
Shankar Brata	Sivaratri, Senjuti Itu, Kulkulti, Bratri Dwitiya	Bhai Phonta and Teohaar
Santoshi Mata	Santoshi Mata, Kalki Narayan, Satyanarayan Barkumar	Santoshi Mata, Rishi Panchami
Santoshi Mata	Kshetra, Tush-Tushli, Santoshi Mata	Santoshi Mata
Lakshmi Brata	Lakshmi Brata, Bhanjo	Kojagar Lakshmi
-	Manik Pir	-
Ganesha Chaturthi	Sankata, Bipattarini, Asan Bibi, Uddhar Bibi Ghaat Kali	-
-	-	-

(Contd.)

(Table Contd.)

Gujarat	*Bangladesh*	*Nepal*
(No rituals in Gujarat till purpose 20)	Saubhagya Chaturthi, Adar Simhasan, Talnavami, Moghini Gacher Gunri,	
	Ambubachi	Rishi Panchami
	Olaichandi, Shirni, Ghentu	
	Sitala, Iatali, Panchra	-
	Puja, Jwarajwuri, Kanu Pir, Shirni, Ghawa Pir etc	
	Banger Biya, Kaker Biya, Badna Pota etc.	-
	Manik Pir	-
	Banabibi, Bana Durga, Dakshin Roy, Baghai etc.	-
	Manasa, Nagpanchami	
	Different Ekadasis, Akshay	-
	Tritia, Aghar Chaturdasi etc.	
Friday (Santoshi Mata)	Thursday (Lakshmi) Friday	
	Santoshi Mata, Tuesday (Mangal Chandi) Saturday (Sani)	-
	Sunday (Ghawa Pir)	

(Contd.)

(Table Contd.)

Gujarat	*Bangladesh*	*Nepal*
Jaya Parvati or Molaket	Sivaratri	-
	Madar Banser Jari, Madarer Loot Kurano	
	Banger Biya, Nalyadaka	
	Ekadasi, Purnima, Amabasya	Ekadasi, Purnima, Amabasya, Sankranti
	Sankranti	
	Dhanya Purnima, Hajir Pir, Kalki Narayan	
	Nauka Puja Brata	

13

Field Survey

Orissa

Source: 1. Rupmini Kundu (62), domestic work. 2. Supriya Panda (38), Journalist 3. Sakuntala Pana (76), household work 4. Gouripada Tripathi (59) teaching: post office and police station, Baripada, Orissa.

Punda Osha: Observed in *Aghrayan* by barren women. Many small pies or a large pie is made and worshipped on the road outside the house. Children are given pies to eat and what is left is eaten by the woman who eats nothing else that day.

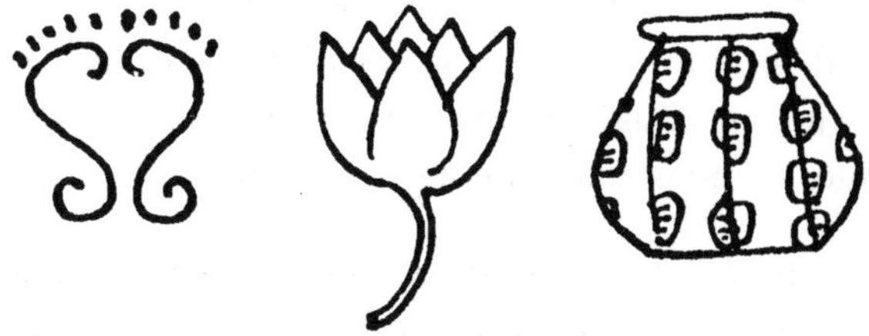

Lakshmi Brata: Married women and widows observe this on each Thursday of *Aghrayan* but not unmarried girls. The narrative that is read makes it clear that cleanliness is an essential part of religion, and that caste barriers should be done away with. Observed for the family's well-being and prosperity.

Samba Dasami Brata: Performed by married women in the month of *Poush.* It is believed that Krishna's son Samba had cured himself of his Leprosy at Konark in Orissa and the ritual is seen as a guard against skin diseases. Worship of the Sun is part of the ritual.

Makar Sankranti Brata: All women observe *Makar Sankranti* in the month of *Poush* by worshipping any deity. There are no restrictions. The prayer is for general well being.

Sudasha Brata: Observed on a Thursday if that happens to be the tenth day of the bright fortnight of that month, generally in *Magh* or *Bhadra.* Ten of each ingredient is needed, like 10 balls of string, 10 flowers, 10 leaves, 10 grains of atap rice. The idea is that observance of the ritual ensures that Lakshmi never leaves that home. The tale has the sage Narada explaining to Indra the significance of the *brata*, after the latter had wanted to know how he would get a wife and sons.

Magh Saptami: Observed on the seventh lunar day of *Magh.* All women and even men can participate.

Siva Chaturdasi Brata: Observed in the month of *Falgun* by both men and women when lamps are lit to Siva in each home and temple. Fourteen types of flowers and fruits are needed and an equal number of strings. The purpose is to encourage farming and cleaning away sins.

Garvanash Sankranti Brata: Married women observed in *Asvin.* Sweets are made kept on banana leaves and taken to the field for feeding Mother Nature. It is related to agriculture.

Durga Sasthi Brata: Performed by men and women during Durga Puja in *Asvin.* Eight types of flowers and strings are needed, the men and women tying the latter to their arms after the ritual is over. Observed to keep away sin.

Jamaisasthi Brata: Observed in *Kartick* by women who have sons-in-law. They are given new clothes and fed sumptously. The purpose is to ensure that the daughters stay happy.

Janmashtami Brata: Observed in *Bhadra.*

Radhashtami Brata: Observed by unmarried girls 15 days after Janmashtami. Eight pieces of *durba* grass, eight leaves of *kul* (a kind of berry) and an equal number of strings are needed.

Kukkuti Brata: Observed in *Bhadra* by married women. Two fish are let into a water filled hole and the ritual performed at night to got children. The making a hole and filling it with water is like the ritual of *Punyipukur* but the purpose is different.

Somnath Brata: Married women observe this by worshipping Siva in *Bhadra* for the wellbeing of husbands and children.

Ananta Brata: Observed by married women on the fourteenth day of the bright fortnight of *Asvin.* Fourteen flowers and fruits are needed as also fourteen pies. The *brata* is observed for fourteen years. A feature of the *brata* is to set adrift a copper snake in a small box. Any married woman getting this will have to perform the ritual whatever her conditions may be.

In addition tribals in the hilly areas observe *Bāndana Brata* on the day after Kali Puja when men worship cattle. Later gifts of chicks are made. They also observe *Damodar Brata* three days after *Makar Sankranti* when by a river or pond the *brati* gives away things used by a dead person and gets in return chicken and rice, which is eaten on the way back. The purpose is to attain heaven.

On the day of *Chaitra Sankranti* (the last day of *Chaitra*) the tribals of Mayurbhanj must hunt and kill at least one animal, so that throughout the year they will have no problems eking out a livelihood. This is called *Akhanda Shikar* or Uninterrupted Hunting.

Bangladesh : Kishoreganj

Source: Pushparani Roy (55), housewife, Bagadia village, P.S. Kishoreganj

Lakshmi Brata: Observed by all women on any Thursday or Sunday of the bright fortnight of *Aghrayan.* There is another Lakshmi *brata* observed by all women. The purpose is to ensure that the new paddy crop is not affected by insects and the paddy is kept in the hollow of banana trunks called 'dol'. After the ritual this is kept in the thatched roof of the hut for a year. The alpana consists of footprints of the deity.

Mangal Chandi: Lakshmi and Narayan are painted with vermillion on banana leaves and a pitcher is kept with five dots of vermillion. Eight leaves of wood-apple, betel-nuts, betel-leaves and the auspicious 'durba' grass are needed, seasonal fruits as also *Chura* (flattened rice) sugar, banana. It is for the well being for the family.

Kanu Pir Brata: Observed on Thursdays or Sundays of the bright fortnight of *Bhadra* by married women and unmarried girls in the afternoon. The purpose is to keep skin diseases away. After the ritual the woman eats only the *mera pitha* (kind of pie) which are among the offerings.

Source: Jharnarani Ghosh (36) housewife, Bagadia village.

Ghawa Pir Brata: Observed on Thursday and Sunday of *Bhadra, Magh* and *Falgun* by women for the cure of ailments. The offerings include three pies which the woman eats after the ritual is performed around noon and nothing else. The next day she can take rice.

Sankattarini Brata: Performed by all women to ward off dangers. It is observed as a *manat* or promise to offer sacrifices after the fulfillment of a prayer.

Manasa Brata.

Manasa Brata: On the day before observing it, the women have to take vegetarian food. The song sung on the occasion says:

"Son to the son less
Wealth to the poor,
Remove all illness and sorrow.
Remember Manasa,
(And) Get enemies
destroyed".

The snake motif is a must in the alpana painted on the occasion.

Baidyanath Brata: The woman fasts the whole day and in the evening keeps some rice in a banana trunk and covers it with another. In another place broken rice, banana, sugar is kept. After the narration is over, the whole thing is mixed with water and given to the woman and children. It is for the good health of husbands and children.

The story of the *brata* is about a Brahmin woman who had no children and so had to face insults from everybody. She was about to commit suicide when Baidyanath Thakur arrived and advised her to worship Baidyanath. She did so and was blessed with a son. She stopped worshipping the deity and the son was covered with skin diseases. He was left in the streets to die but again the deity arrived, advised him to worship him and he was cured.

Source: Niharkana Roy (65), housewife, Binnagaon village, Kishoreganj.

Karmapurush Brata: A ritual observed by men on the last day of *Jaistha.* The offering is a lump of sweets, bananas and *khoi,* or parched rice and a hole is filled with curd. It is a ritual than runs through generations to remember forefathers.

Sasthi Brata: Observed by women for the children's well being. The offering is a mixture of parched rice, curd, flattened rice, sweets and bananas given on a jackfruit leaf.

Sani Brata: Observed on all Saturdays, in a big way in *Baisakh* and *Jaistha* when a mixture is prepared of broken rice, or wheat flour, sugar, bananas, milk and fruits, which is called 'sinni'. An iron ring and new clothes are also offered. After the ceremony a winnow is beaten and the 'sinni' distributed among all.

Gacher Gunri Brata (Tree Trunk brata): Observed during a marriage by married women. Alpana is painted and a branch of the 'sheora', a wild tree, is planted. Parched rice, sugar, and bananas with seeds are needed. Purpose is to resist evil spirits.

Bipadnashini Brata: Observed on Fridays by woman to get rid of troubles.

Nabanna: Performed by all women in *Aghrayan* or *Poush* on the day of the full moon. Sweets and pies of the newly harvested rice are made.

Kartick Brata: Observed by widows.

Sitala: As a protection against small-pox.

Jwarajwari Brata: Observed when fevers occur on a large scale.

Source: Usharani Devi(46) teacher, Batris village, Kishoreganj; Mohammad Saidur (57), engaged in folk research with Bangla Academy, Batris village, Kishoreganj.

Garsi Brata: To drive away 'Alakshmi' or the force against Lakshmi and pay respects to the dead mother-in-law. It is observed on the last day of *Asvin*. A pond is made in the courtyard, a basil tree planted and images of clay have to be made, one of an elderly woman with child in arms, another of 'Alakshmi' with long nails and hair which will be made to lie on a banana leaf. Eight types of vegetables and pulses will have to be kept along with fruits. During the ritual a part of the vegetables and pulses will have to be dropped in the pond and the rest cooked and eaten after the ceremony and also distributed. The water with which a hole is filled to make the pond must include coconut water. The ritual is also called *Yama Pukur Brata*.

Hajir Pir Brata: Observed by Muslim women to get back things lost. The 'sinni' or mixture of rice, wheat flour, sugar, fruits has to be made and betel-leaves and betel-nuts are also needed. While lostening to the tale of the ritual, the women are supposed to chew betel-leaves and spit out the juice.

Kshetra Brata: Tale is about a king's daughter who was married off to a day labourer as the king had promised one day that she would be married to the man he would see first the next day. They had a small plot of land which the wife tilled and when the paddy was ripe for harvesting asked her husband to do so. However, the more he harvested the more paddy grew and at last seven figures appeared and told him that he had been blessed by them and would receive more blessings if he observed the *Kshetra Brata* when the new paddy arrived every year. The ingredients they told him were, seven pies, dried fish, bananas, molasses etc.

Performed after harvesting in the month of *Aghrayan*. Those who observe the *brata* cannot eat the new rice till they have completed it.

Rath Brata/Rathai Chandi: Observed in the month of *Asaṛh* on the day of the Chariot Festival. Attendance to it must be preceded by this ritual. Portions of parched and flattened rice and fruits are kept on a banana leaf and each portion has to be eaten by a member of the family. Fasting before the ritual is a must and additional merit is earned if the fast is continued till the chariot is touched or the rope pulled.

The story is about two sisters, Rathai and Kathai. The first was married to a rich man who did not believe in religion or rituals and how on the day of the festival he and his family had fallen by the roadside. They were revived by Kathai with water she was carrying for her own performance of the ritual. The husband of Rathai then spread the message of the *brata* as essential to keep the body going.

Chhaya (six) Sasthi Brata: The sixth after the birth of a baby is called *Chhaya Sasthi* night when the infant's fate is decided. The ritual is observed in the evening and a maternal uncle or some relative must be present to hear it. Also somebody has to stay awake the whole night in the room where the mother sleeps with the baby.

The purpose of the *brata* is to keep happy Chitragupta who decides the fates of human beings. No fasting is required. The maternal uncle is important because in the tale of the ritual it was one such person who had come to know from Chitragupta what fate lay ahead for his two nephews and niece and helped them overcome their problems when they grew up.

Sumati Brata: Observed to help good intentions drive away the bad. Can be performed on any Monday or Friday. After bathing in the morning the women will have to go out in her wet clothes and collect rice from five homes. This rice is offered in the ritual along with betel-leaves, oil and vermillion, which are given to married women. It is also observed for marriage of daughters getting on in years.

Subachani (incarnation of Durga) *Brata:* For wealth and children.

Mangal Chandi (incarnation of Durga): Can be observed either in Baisakh or in *Jaistha* to ged rid of ill luck and the family's well-being.

Santoshi Mata (Daughter of Ganesha): For good luck and the power to shake off all fears.

Barkumar Brata: The story is of a king who had no children and going by superstition people refused to see his face as that they feared would bring bad luck. One day a beggar came to the palace, saw the king and gave him a banana saying if the queen ate the fruit she would deliver a son. The beggar was Barkumar in disguise. A son was born and the queen began worshipping Barkumar. One day, however, when there was a function in the palace she forgot and the son died. The king and queen were inconsolable when Barkumar again appeared and brought the child back to life.

It is family ritual, observed before any happy occasion like marriage or the first day the child takes rice. Men can also participate but if it is observed once it must be kept up.

Source: Rinarani Sarkar (40) housewife, Damiha village, Tarail police station, Kishoreganj.

Punai or Maghi Purnima Brata: Observed on the full moon night of *Magh* by married women for family peace. The ingredients include five types of pies and five types of vegetable dishes and rice. The deity to whom the offerings are made is Laksmi. A hole is dug and filled with water to represent a pond in which a black fish of the carp family is released. After the ritual the women tear off hay from the thatched roof and burn these at a three-lane crossing.

Sankranti Brata: Also observed for peace and happiness at noon on Thursday of any month. The ingredients are, clay pot, mango branch with five leaves, flower, incense, vermillion, flowers, sugar etc. The woman observing the ritual will make three pies of broken rice and eat these secretly after the ceremony—the first she will eat in a kneeling pose, the second with her head down and the last bringing her hand up to her mouth from below the right knee.

The story is about a woman who on her marriage night and told her husband about her faith in *Sankartani*. The husband did not believe in such things and in anger threw away her ornaments in the river. She did not what to do and fell asleep in her dream the deity appeared and told her the ornaments would be in the stomach of a fish which her father-in-law would bring the next day for the marriage feast. This was what happened, the husband ultimately realised his mistake and the *brata* began to be observed with reverence.

Ekachora Barkumar Brata: Observed on any Saturday at noon for male children, wealth and peace. Either the cowshed or a room will have to be purified with cowdung water and then alpana painted in the centre of which a pitcher is placed and the ingredients kept before it. These are five mango leaves, flower sandalwood paste, sugar, molasses etc.

The story is the same as that of the *Barkumar Brata,* of how a couple gets a son with the blessings of Barkumar then forgets to worship him and the son died, only to be revived by the deity when the couple realised their mistake.

Source: Sanatanchandra Burman (70), farmer, Damiha village, Tarail police station, Kishoreganj.

Gorakshanath Brata: Performed by men 21 days after a calf is born to their cow. The animal is milked and in the evening the rituals are performed in front of the cowshed. It is the good health of cattle who continue to be used for agriculture.

Source: Prafulla Chandra Sarkar (60) businessman, Damiha village, Tarail police station, Kishoreganj

Kalkinarayan Brata: Observed by men for getting back lost property. children for those women who don't have any and cure of illness.

Source: Kunjalata Sarkar (70), housewife, Damiha village, Tarail police station, Kishoreganj.

Maski Brata (Bandurga Brata): It is for the well being of a new mother and her baby. It has similarities with the Bandurga Brata. To save the mother and the baby from evil spirits, neem leaves, a broken chopper, a broomstick are kept next to their head and incense burnt in the room. After 30 days the mother wears new clothes and carrying the things needed for the *brata* goes to a 'sheora' tree (wild tree) where these are put down. There she ties a red bracelet to the leaves of the tree, make two dolls of rice-paste, break the egg of a duck and place the yellow portion between the two. The shell is then filled with water and then she emoraces the tree. While returning, neither she nor anybody else will lock back as that will invite ill luck.

Back home the mother is fed rice with five vegetables and the baby is dressed in new clothes after the barber shaves the head.

Netrakona

Source: Dipalirani Sarkar (40), housewife, Kendua Bazar village, Kendua police station, Netrakona district.

Ghawa Pir Brata: For curing illness. The *bratini* has to fast and bring home paddy begged from five homes. She husks the paddy in a mortar and pestle made of wood, grounds the rice thus got and mass three pies from those. It can be performed on any Thursday or Sunday afternoon.

Paddy, banana, sugar and molasses are needed for the *brata.* After the ceremony the *bratini* will eat the three pies but nothing at night.

The story is of a poor family whose son developed sores in the body which nobody could cure. He began to small and was left by the river side. There he was found by a man and a woman who asked him to roll over in the hot sand bank of the river and then to bathe rubbing himself with sand and mud. He did that was cured and the man told him he was Ghawa Pir (*gha* means sore) and the woman was his wife and that he should be worshipped.

The son went with them and returned home after a long time. When he told his parents what had happened to him, they decided to observe the Ghawa Pir Brata every month.

Source of songs for Manasi Brata: Dipalirani Sarkar (40), housewife. Kendua Gram Village, Kendua police station, Netrakona.

The *brata* has already been discussed. Since it is closely related to the *Gacher Guṅti* (tree trunk) and *Bandurga bratas,* the women refer to those while singing their way to the 'sheora' trees. At first the song is about Radha going to meet 'Krishna' under the 'Kadamba' tree meaning the women going to the 'sheora' tree with a chorus providing the refrain "Radhe Saijja Chaley Go", meaning "Radha goes all dressed up." Then the woman sings about meeting Vana Durga at the *sheora* tree, worshipping her and making friends with her all of which she narrates to her mother-in-law.

The last part of the song is sung as the *bratini* and the other rowman return home. The return journey is considered, in the song, as akin to Madhab (Krishna) rowing back Radha in his boat and at one stage she also reminds him that she is her maternal aunt. A touch of contemporaneity is provided by the lines which speak of saris having been bought and kept in a locked suitcase. It ends with a description of the "donerful sight in the garden, two friends (the woman and the tree) embracing and exchanging vermillion among themselves.

Jessore

Source: 1. Krishna Bakshi (70), housewife, Jalisa police station, Magura.

2. Putulrani Maitra (50), housewife, Rashkhali village, Magura.

Aukshoy Ghat Brata: Observed in Baisakh to ensure that there is never any shortage of water. On the auspicious day of *Aukshoy Tritia*, a pitcher is filled with water, mango leaves placed at the mouth and the vessel decorated with vermillion and sandalwood. Fruits, sweets, the sacred thread (*paita*), coins and a leaf fan are kept on a earthen plate and the pitcher and other things donated to a Brahmin. The number goes up to two in the second year, three in the third and four in the fourth year. The Brahmin from whom the vow is originally taken is given a silver or brass pot.

Fal Gachano Brata: It is believed that those who observe this *brata* never have to bother about food. The rituals have to be performed for a month and early in the morning from the last day of *Chhaitra*. It has to be observed for four years and donations of fruits, sweets and coins made to Brahmins. During the *brata*, thirteen Brahmins have to be fed and given, if possible, clothes, umbrellas and sweets. If conditions do not permit this then gifts are given only to the Brahmin who had first administered the vow.

Tal Navami Brata: Observed in the ninth day (*navami*) of the bright fortnight of *Bhadra* to earn the love of husbands. Sitting in his heavenly abode (*Baikuntha Dham*) Narayan was supposed to have told Lakshmi of the *brata*. The ritual involves offerings to Narayan, feeding Brahmins and the husband and then eating from the same plate. Nine types of fruits, flowers, sweets and incense are needed and the Brahmin has to be given a *dhoti* and a rupee.

Comilla

Source: Maya Das (64), housewife, Ratnabati village, Comilla district.

Maghmandal: Unmarried girl observe this throughout the month of *Magh*. After her bath, the girl prepares a colour mixing rice-paste, chaff, powdered brick etc and draws a large circle in the courtyard representing Earth. Inside the circle, the sun, the moon, human and animal figures are drawn. Then songs to the merit of sun and moon worship are sung. The purpose is to have good hasbands, peace and prosperity.

Dola Brata: Observed by married women a month after *Maghmandal* for financial comfort. After fasting the whole day, a palanquin (*dola*) with two bearers has to be painted in the evening and a rhyme recited. It says:

"As I worship a clay dola
(So) May I have a gold dola".

Bhai Phonta: Observed on the second day of the bright fortnight of *Kartick* for brothers' well being. The rhyme speaks of the *brata* saving the brother from *Yama.*

Motif Index in Brata Narrations

As we have seen the observance of no *brata* is complete unless the *brati* or *bratini* listens to the tale associated with it and the narration of which is an integral part of the whole ritual. These tales enjoy similarity with fables and folk tales. Every folk tale has one or more themes which are identified as motifs and which can be found in the *brata* in tales.

The motifs as identified in Stith Thompson's 'Motif Index if Folk Literature' which is in six volumes:

A 21.1 Creator of man and woman

A 123.2.1.2 Four-faced deity

A 123.5.1 Deity with many arms

A 124.1 Deity with fiery eyes

A 131 Deity with animal shape

A 132 Deity in the shape of animal

A 133 Deity in the shape of demon

A 136.1.3 Deity on a bull

A 136.1.4.1 Deity on swan

A 136.1.6 Deity on buffalo (Yama)

A 136.1.7 Deity on lion

A 155.5 Divine elephant

A 156 Priceless treasure of the deity

A 156.5 Deity's chariot

A 162 Conflict among deities

A 162.1 Battle between deities and demons

A 164.7 Parvati

A 165.7 Paṛvati

A 165.2 Divine messenger

A 425 Deity as a male river

A 425.1 Deity as female river

A 454.1 Goddess of Cure

A 462.1 Goddess of Beauty

A 463 Goddess of Fate

A 464 God of Justice

A 473.1 Goddess of Wealth

A 478.2 Goddess of Small Pox (Sitala)

A 482.1 God if Ill Fortune

A 482.2 God of Fortune

A 487 God of Death

A 661 Heaven

B 11.2.3.1 Snake with seven hoods

B 41.2 Pegasus

B 101.7 Snake with gem on its hood

B 120 Clever Animal

B 122.0.4 Parrot who forecasts the future

B 122.1 Counselling Bird

B 143 Wise Bird

B 211.3.1 Talking Owl

B 211.4 Talking Cat

B 240.4 Lion

B 240.5 Tiger

B 280 Animal's Marriage

B 411 Helpful Cow

B 557.3 Tiger carrying man on its back

B 557.3 Cat acting as man's carrier

B 581.1 Bird giving wealth to man

B 776.7 Poisonous Snake

C 50 Annoying the Deity

C 331 Looking Back

C 420 Revealing Secret

C 435.1 Uttering Husband's Name

C 920.1 Death of Son for Disobeying Ban

D 42.2 She Demon in guise of Woman

D 42.3 Demon in Man's shape

D 97 Transformation from human to witch

D 800 Object secured by magic

D 811 Getting such an object from a deity

D 812.1 Getting it from a sanyasi

D 967 Magic Root

D 1347 Magic Material lends fertility

D 1347.3 Magic Medicine makes barren woman pregnant

D 1652.3.1 wish fulfilling cow

D 1812.3.3 Seeing the future in dreams

D 1814.2 Getting guidance in dream

E 0 Rebirth

E 600 New Life

E 611.5.1 Deity is born as a cat

F 11 Travelling in air

F 16 Journey to the moon

F Travel to the animal kingdom in the nether world

F 200 Fairy

F 370 Journey to fairy land

F 582.1 Daughter of Shake

F 827.5 Golden Comb

F 846.2 Golden Bed

G 11.6 Maneater Woman

155 Wisdom from woman

J 157 Wisdom in Dream

J 1112 Clever wife

J 1705 Brahmin

J 1705.3 Stupid Fisherman

J 1705.5 Miser

J 2160 Carelessness about Consequence

K 300.1 Thief

K 311.4.1 Cheat in guise of Saint

K 735 To Entrap

K 2110.1 Criticised Wife

K 2212.2 Treacherous Sister of Husband

L 111.3 Widow's Son a Hero

L 419.1 King becomes Pauper

M 205 Breaking vow

M 411.14.3 Curse of Brahmin

N 101 Cruel Fate

N 141 Fate and intelligence: Which is stronger

N 203.1 Fortunate Woman

N 250 Ill Fate

N 831 Woman Assistant

P 16.4.1 Chaste Woman

P 253 Brother and Sister

Q 2 Kind and Heartless

Q 20 Prize for Just Conduct

Q 33 Prize for Good Behaviour

Q 45 Prize for Hospitality

Q 51 Prize for kindness to animals

Q 220 Punishment for Irreligious Act

Q 223 Punishment for ignoring Gods

Q 276 Punishment for Greed

Q 331 Punishment for Vanity

Q 560 Suffering in Hell

S 3L Cruel Stepmother

S 51 Cruel Mother-in-law

S 410 Tortured Wife

T 53 Matchmaker

T 511.1 Pregnant after eating fruit

T 511.2.01 Pregnant after eating roots

T 685 Twins

W 11 Generosity

W 11.2 Kind King

W 154 Gratitude

Z 71.2 Numerical Sign : Four

Z 71.8 Numerical Sign : Twelve

Z 71.9 Numerical Sign : Thirteen

Z 72.1 Twelve years thirteen days

by
Charubala Deb

Biskram Brata's Alpana

List of Popular Bratas Observed in India

Aamsasthi
Abighnakar
Acala Ekadashi
Acambitpir
Adahalud
Adarsimhasan
Aghor Caturdasi
Ahoi Astami
Aiappa
Aja Ekadashi
Akashpradeep
Akhand Dwadasi
Akhand Shikar Brata
Akhti
Akhyateej
Akshay Phal
Akshaykumari
Akshaynavami
Akshaytritia
Akulanir Brata
Alakshmi
Aleri
Amabasya
Ambubaci
Amla Navami
Amlaki Ekadashi
Amoji Pankha
An Noan Karna
Anant
Anantcaturdasi
Andhasasthi
Andheswari
Annakut
Annasasthi
Arandhan
Aranyasasthi
Arfa
Arogya Saptami
Arundhati
Asanbibi
Asanpirer Brata
Asha Bhagvati
Ashamai
Ashmata
Ashok

Ashoka Sasthi
Ashtalokapal
Asibar
Asipatra
Astami
Asvatha Pata
Asvinikumar
At Anaj
Ateshwar
Atriganga Navami
Aula Khadini
Aul-Caul Khunti Cor
Baba Kudroburo
Bachar Bayas
Bada Shankolir Brata
Badam Har
Badi Teej
Badnapota
Baghai
Baghrai
Bahumahala
Baibhab Lakshmi
Baidyanath

Baisakhi Trayadashi
Bajbaras
Bakpancak
Baldurga
Balitritiya
Baman Ekadashi
Bandana Brata
Baram
Baripuja
Barkumar
Barlakshmi
Barmatam
Barsayat Amabasya
Baruni Snan
Baruthini Ekadashi
Basanda
Basantrai
Basnara
Basudhara
Basuli
Bateshvara
Bauluka
Belbhata

Belpukur
Betai Candi
Bhabhuta Siddha
Bhadai
Bhaduli
Bhaghai Sirni
Bhagria
Bhagwanpat
Bhaianduj
Bhaibeej
Bhaiduj
Bhaimi Ekadasi
Bhanjo
Bhenpu
Bherunpuja Brata
Bhimapuja
Bhisma Pancak
Bhisu
Bhogi Pongal
Bhojali or Bhujaria
Bholapoda
Bhoot Chaturdasi
Bhratri Dwitiya

Bidhatrisasthi

Bidri

Bijoya Ekadashi

Bijoyadasami

Bindayak

Bipattarini

Birinci

Bishari

Brahman

Brata

Brikshapuja

Budhai Osa

Budhi Teej

Budi Adananda

Buranuri

Byanger Biya

Caiti Mangalbar Osa

Caitra lakshmi

Caitrabaruni

Caitranavami

Caitrasankranti

Caitrashukla Pratipada

Caitri Amabasya

Caitsatuani

Camar Jhi

Campak Caturdasi

Campasasthi

Candi

Candrasasthi

Candrayan

Capra Sasthi

Champa Chandan

Chat Brata

Chatak

Chatua Sankranti

Chay Sasthi

Chetra

Choti Teej

Choto Brata

Cidiyamuthi

Cilai Brata

Cungir Brata

Dadhisankranti

Dadhisankranti

Daibauthani

Dakshinroy

Dalan Pir

Damodar

Darpan Darshan

Darpansankranti

Dashara

Dashmata or Dashrani

Dasputtal

Debathani Ekadashi

Debshani Ekadashi

Deulpuja Brata

Devsuni

Dhan Brata

Dhanteras

Dhanyapurnima

Dharma

Dhelaphela

Dhulasasthi

Dhundko Neg Brata

Dhupsankranti

Diwali

Doas

Dola Brata

Dolgaras

Dubadisat

Duitibahan

Durbashtami

Durga or Bodhansasthi

Dusshera

Ekacor Barkumar Brata

Ekadasi

Ekul Okul Puja Brata

Ekusyassthi

Eosankranti

Falgun Trayadashi

Gach-Beej Pujan

Gacher Gundi Brata

Gadai

Gadashi

Gaji Pir

Gajir Bans Uthana

Gajiyabhar

Gajjabrata

Ganeshcaturthi

Gangadashhara

Ganganavami

Gangapancami

Ganga-Yamuna

Gaoa Pir

Garba

Garvana Sankranti

Gathe Mangal

Ghadulia

Ghaila Brata

Ghantakarna

Ghatkali

Ghatpat

Ghritasamkranti

Ghulandi

Girirajbrata

Go Kshur

Goapuja Brata

Gobardhan

Gobatsa Dvadashi

Gobatsa Ekadashi

Goganavami

Gokal

Gorakshanath Seva

Gordhan or Madai

Gosthasasthi

Gotaseddha

Gouritritia

Govinda Dwadasi

Gudumacuka

Guga Pancami

Guptadhan

Guri Paroa

Gurupurnima

Hajirpir

Halasasthi

Halchat

Haldi Kumkum

Halpuja

Hareli or Hariri

Hari Amabasya

Haripancak

Hariparameshvarer

Harir Charan

Harishayani Ekadashi

Harishmangal Candi

Haritalika

Hartal Teej

Hat Ghurni	Jatakasasthi	Kalka
Hauola	Jatak-Bhatkar	Kalkinarayan
Hidali	Jaya-Parvati	Kalurai
Holi Ka Bulendi	Jaylakumari	Kamaksha
Holika Pujan	Jaymangalbar	Kamida Ekadashi
Hrishipancami	Jeevatputtika	Kamkhat
Illighungir Brata	Jethan Bhet	Kanjiamla
Indira Ekadashi	Jhanda	Kanu Pir
Indurer Bia	Jhatpat	Kanubhai
Irshawali	Jhatpat Thakur	Kapardi Vinayak
Itu	Jhirmir	Karam
Itulakshmi	Jhulan	Karamgunsai
Iyatali	Jitashtami	Karba Atham
Jagar	Jiyatkali	Karmadi
Jahni	Jvarasura	Karmadwityer Brata
Jaistha Campak	Jwarajuri	Karmapuruser Brata
Jalsasthi	Kadali Sasthi	Kartik
Jamaisasthi	Kajari Purnima	Kartik Snan
Jamaisasthi	Kajliteej	Kartiker Lakshmi
Janki or Sitashtami	Kak Brata	Kartikeya
Janmashtami	Kaker Bia	Kartiki Purnima
Jaoara	Kalathakurer Brata	Karwa Cauth
Jarag	Kalbhairab	Katyani

Kaua Magan Brata
Kaura-Kauri
Khauapirer Brata
Khedai Thakur Brata
Khoajer Dinga Bhasan
Khoajkhijir
Khoicera
Khoidai
Khudurkuni Osa
Kodasasthi
Kojagari Lakshmi
Kokila Brata
Kokmar
Kolabibir Sirni
Komai
Kothamuthi
Krishna Ekadashi
Krishnasasthi
Kshetra
Kshetrapal
Kujalaya
Kukkuti
Kulaithakurer Brata
Kulanamano
Kulkar Mangalcandi
Kulkuti
Kuloghat
Kuluimangalcandi
Kumar Purnima
Kumirpuja
Kushadapadani
Kushe Ausi
Lalita
Lalitasaptami
Lalu
Lapshitapasir Brata
Lohri
Lotan
Ma Dumni
Ma Gotha
Madar Banser Jari
Madhu or
Madhusankranti
Madhushravani
Magadheshwai Seva
Magha
Maghabrata
Maghipurnima
Maghisnan
Maghmandal
Maghneshvari
Mahadana
Mahakali
Mahalakshmi
Mahanavami
Makal
Makar Sankranti
Malyapir
Mamulia
Manasa
Mangal Chandi
Mangala Gouri
Manikpir
Manlag
Manorath Dwitiya
Manvantara
Marudagna
Maski Brata
Masoprobas

Maswa
Mathanisasthi
Mattu Pongal
Mauni Amabashya
Mecheni Tistabudi
Megharanir Brata
Meghnad
Meleni
Midibidi
Milimai
Mohini Ekadashi
Mokshada Ekadashi
Mounabrati Ekadashi
Mula Sasthi
Musafir
Mushkil Asan
Nikat Mangalcandi
Nabanna
Nabasatbatsar
Nagcousi
Nagpancami
Nakdhatra
Nakhchut
Nalyadaka
Nanad Brata
Narak Caturdashi
Narayan
Narayan-Tadayaner
Natai
Naukapuja
Naurat or Jaoria
Nauratas
Navabarsha Brata
Navaratra
Navratri
Neel Sasthi
Nilkul Vasudeva
Nimanikanti
Nirakali
Nirakul Prameshvari
Nirjala Ekadashi
Niskalanka
Nistarini
Nityasinhur
Niura Moumi
Niyamseva Brata
Nrisimha Caturdasi
Olai Candi
Onam
Padma Ekadashi
Padmapurnima
Pancabhikshuk
Pancananda
Panckumar
Pancrapuja
Pancuka
Pandum
Panyasankranti
Papankushi Ekadashi
Parad
Pasan Caturdasi
Pataisasthi
Patal Phond
Pati Brata
Patidurgamata
Paushsankranti
Pavandevatar Puja Brata
Pavitra Ekadashi

Pencapenci
Phagunkuna
Phaldan
Phalgachan
Phoolpati
Pipalpathai
Pous Amaos
Poushlakshmi
Prabadhani Ekadashi
Prados
Prithvi
Pukh-Nakshatra
Punai or Maghi Purnima Brata
Punde Osa
Punyipukur
Purada Ekadashi
Purnima
Radhahtami
Raidamodar
Rajsankranti
Rakhipurnima
Rakshabandhan
Rakshamangal
Rama Ekadashi
Ramnavami
Rane Eo
Rath or Rathai Candi
Renchda
Rohin
Roophalud
Roshni
Rupasi
Sachapan
Safala Ekadashi
Sakath Couth
Samaytrani
Sambadashami
Sampaddor
Sandhyamani
Sanir Pancali
Sanja Puja
Sanjha
Sankata
Sankatatarini
Sankranti
Santan Navami
Santoshi Mata
Saratpurnima
Sarpapuja
Sasthi
Sater Lakshmi
Satiya Amabasya
Satpanchami
Satpuja
Sattila Ekadashi
Satyanarayan
Satyapir
Satyapir
Saubhagya Caturthi
Savitri
Sejuti
Setera or Sutikasasthi
Sankarttani Brata
Shibaji Brata
Silnora Puja Brata
Shirag
Sitala Astami
Sitalasasthi

Siva
Sradhapitraraksha
Sravan Shukla
Shravani
Sukbhanta
Shyamji
Siddheshvari
Siddhivinayak
Sitala
Sithicad
Sivamushti
Sivaratri
Solokala
Somnath
Somvati Amabasya
Sondar
Sri Pancami
Subacani
Sudasha
Sukharatri
Sumati
Suo Duo
Surajsaptami

Surya
Surya Pongal
Suryasasthi
Sutikasasthi
Talnavami
Talnavami
Tara
Tarabhojan
Tarabhojan
Taran
Tariamander Brata
Teej
Tejdarpan
Thakthaki
Thanki Thakrun
Thua
Tian
Tijayat
Tikka
Tilakjari
Tilkumari
Tisua Sombar
Tisumata Puja Brata

Tosla Mishtasankranti
Trayadasi
Tribhuvan Caturthi
Trinather Seva Brata
Tush Tushli
Tushu
Udaymangal
Udaymangal
Uddharbibi
Ugadi
Uma Maheswar
Upangalalita
Utpanna Ekadashi
Vaikuntha Caturdasi
Van Bibi
Vanbeduno
Vandurga
Varada Caturthi
Vasant Budi
Vasantpancami
Vastubibi
Vastupuja Brata
Veerashtami

Vikrami Baisakh Sankranti

Vishkaram

Vishnupuja

Vivaha Pancami

Vivahasasthi

Vivaswapt Saptami

Vyaspurnima

Yamadwitiya

Yampukur

Yudla

Bibliography

English

Aarne, A. and Thompson, S. : Types of the Folk-Tale (FFC No. 74; Helsinki, 1929).

Ahuja, D.R. : Folklore of Rajasthan (New Delhi, 1994).

Anand, Subhash : Major Hindu Festivals (Bombay, 1991).

Balys, Jones & Thompson, Stith : The Oral Tales of India (Bloomington, 1958).

Bangladesh Bureau of Statistics : Statistical Yearbook of Bangladesh 1994 (Dhaka 1995).

Bapat, Tara : Rituals and Festivals of India (Bombay, 1992).

Bascom, William R. : Contributions to Folkloristics (Meerut, 1986).

Beck, Brendra E.F., Clans : Folktales of India (Delhi, 1989).

Bedi, Sohinder Singh : Folklore of the Punjab (New Delhi, 1991).

Ben-Amos, Dan : Folklore Context Essays (New Delhi, 1982).

Bhattacharya, S.K. : Folk Heritage of India (Varanasi, 1989).

—Folk Literature of the World (Varanasi, 1989).

Bodding, P.O. : Santal Foktale. 3 Vols. (Oslo and Cambridge, Mass, 1925-29).

Bompas, Cecil Henry : Folklore of the Santal Parganas (New Delhi, 1981).

Chaudhuri, A.B. : The Santals, Religions and Rituals (New Delhi, 1987).

Chettiar, S.M.L. Lakshmanan : Folklore of Tamil Nadu (New Delhi 1991).

Crafts Council of West Bengal : The Arts of Bengal and Eastern India (Calcutta, 1982).

Dalton, E.T. : Descriptive Ethnology of Bengal (Calcutta, 1872).

Dange, Mrs. Sindhu S. : Hindu Domestic Rituals (New Delhi, 1985).

Das, K.B. & Mahapatra L.K. : Folklore of Orissa (New Delhi, 1993).

Dundes Alan : Essays in Folkloristics (Meerut, 1978).

—Folklore Matters (University of Tennessee Press, 1989).

Dutt, Gurusaday : Folk Arts and Crafts of Bengal : The Collected Papers (Calcutta, 1990).

—The Folk Dance of Bengal (Calcutta, 1954).

Enthoven, R.E. : Folklore Notes, Vol. 1, Folklore of Konkon (Delhi, 1915).

Frazer, Sir James George : The Golden Bough, Abridged Edn, (New York, 1963).

Gimbutas, Mariya : The Language of the Goddess (New York, 1989).

Goldstein, Kenneth S. : A guide for Field Workers in Folklore (Pennsylvania, 1964).

Gupte, B.A. : Hindu Holidays and Ceremonials (Calcutta, 1916).

Hafiz, Abdul, Edt. : Folk Tales of Bangladesh (Dhaka, 1985).

Handoo, Jawaharlal Edt : Folklore of Rajasthan (Mysore, 1983).

Islam, Mazharul : Folklore : The Pulse of the People (New Delhi, 1985).

—The Theoretical Study of Folklore (Dhaka, 1998).

Kuisley, David : Hindu Goddesses (Delhi, 1987).

Kuper, Adam & Kuper Jessica Edt : The Social Science Encyclopaedia (New York, 1996).

Leach, Maria, Edt. : Standard Dictionary of Folklore, Mythology, and Legend (in One Vol). (New York, 1984).

Leslie, Lulia Edt. : Roles and Rituals for Hindu Women (Delhi, 1992).

Mittoo, Harikrishan : Himachal Pradesh (New Delhi, 1993).

Panikkar, Kavalam Narayana : Folklore of Kerala (New Delhi, 1991).

Parmar, Shyam : Folklore of Madhya Pradesh (New Delhi,1992).

Paulsen, Kathryn : The Complete Book of Magic Witch of Craft. (England, 1980).

Publications Division : Festivals of India (New Delhi,1992).

Risley, H.H. : The Tribes and Castes of Bengal. Vol. 1 & II (Calcutta, 1891).

Roberts, Warren E. and Stith Thompson: Types of Indic Oral Tales (FFC No. 180; Helsinki, 1965).

Roy Choudhury, P.C. : Folklore of Bihar (New Delhi, 1976).

Roy Sudhansu Kumar : The Ritual Art of the Bratas of Bengal (Calcutta, 1961).

Sengupta, Sankar : Folklore of Bengal—A Projected Study (Calcutta, 1976).

Siddique, Ashraf : Our Folklore Our Heritage (Dhaka,1977).

Singh, Ajit Kumar : Tribal Festivals of Bihar (New Delhi, 1982).

Sivananda, Swami : Hindu Fasts and Festivals (U.P. 1993).

Thompson, Stith : Motif-Index of Folk-Literature Vol. I-VI (Indiana, 1957).

Vatuk, Ved Prakas : Studies in Indian Folk Traditions (New Delhi, 1979).

Walker, Barbara G. : The Woman's Encyclopedia of Myths & Secrets (New York, 1983).

Bengali

Adhikary, Indubhasan Edited : Lokadharma Atit O Bartaman (Calcutta, 1959).

Ahmed, Wakil : Banglar Lokasanskriti (Dhaka, 1974).

Aldin, Selim: Madhyayuger Bangla Natya (Dhaka, 1996).

Annapurna Devi: Mayeder Bratakatha (Collection, Calcutta, 1333).

Asgar, Saikat : Gurusaday Dutta (Bibliography, Dhaka, 1994).

Bandopadhyaya, Amiya Kumar : Bangalakshmir Jhampi (Kolkata, 1386).

Bandopadhyaya, Jitendranath : Panchopasana (Kolkata, 1994).

Bandopadhyaya, Subhash : Pashchim Seemanta Banger Loka Sahitya (Kolkata, 1969).

Baskey, Dhirendranath : Banga Sanskritite Prak Vaidik Probhab (Kolkata, 1992); Adibasi Samaj (First Volume, Kolkata, 1993).

Basu, Gopendra Krishna : Banglar Loukik Devata (Kolkata, 1996).

Basu, Maladhar : Sri Krishna Vijaya (Ed. Khagendra Nath Mitra, Kolkata, 1944).

Bhattacharya Rameshwar : Shivasankirtanpala (Ed, Joginath Halder, Kolkata, 1957).

Bhattacharya Surendra Mohan : Purohit Darpan (Kolkata, 1393).

Bhattacharya, Asutosh : Baish Kabir Manasamangal (Ed. Kolkata, 1962).

—Baglar Lokasahitya, First Volume, (Kolkata, 1962).

—Second Volume (1953).

—Fourth Volume (1966).

Bhattacharya, Bamdeb : Meyeder Bratakatha (Kolkata, 1993).

Bhattacharya, Hansanarayan : Hinduder Debdebi (Kolkata, First Volume 1976, Second Volume 1978, Third Volume 1986).

Bhattacharya, Himadrishankar and Bhattacharya, Sudhishankar: Cochbeharer Prachin Bratakatha (Bardhaman, 1983).

Bhattacharya, Shivaprasad : Bharatiya Sahitye Baramasya (Kolkata, 1959).

Bhattacharya, Sudhi Bhusan Ed. : Dwijamadhabchandra Birachita Mangalchandir Geet (Kolkata, 1965).

Bhattacharya, Sushil Kumar : Uttar Banger Lokasahitya O Sanskriti (Kolkata, 1970).

Bhattacharya, Tarundeb : Purulia (Kolkata, 1986).

Bhowmik Sarita : Paraber Anginaye (Kolkata, 1982).

Bhowmik, Nirmalendu : Bangla Chharar Bhumika (Kolkata, 1979).

Bhuiyan Iqbal Ed. : Nirbachita Rachana Abdul Karim Sahitya Bisharad (Dhaka, 1994).

Chakravarti, Chintaharan : Bhasa Sahitya O Sanskriti (Kolkata, 1993).

Chakravarti, Ghanaram : Sri Dharma Mangal (Edited by Piyush Kanti Mahapatra, Kolkata, 1961).

Chakravarti, Mukundaram : Chandi Mangal (Sahitya Academi, Kolkata, 1969).

Chakravarti, Sunil : Lokayat Bangla (Kolkata, 1969).

Chattopadhyaya, Aghorenath : Meyeli Brata (Ed. Srilekha Chattopadhyay, Kolkata, 1997).

Chowdhurani, Sarala Devi : Jibaner Jharapata (Kolkata, 1982).

Chowdhury, Abul Ahsan Ed. : Abdul Karim Sahitya Bisarad Rachanabali (Dhaka, 1997).

Chowdhury, Dulal : Bangar Loka Utsav (Kolkata, 1985).

Chowdhury, Jyotirindranath, Dutta Chowdhury, Sunirmal, Bhattacharya, Amalendu, Bhattacharya, Manabendra : Srihatta-Kachharer Praching Itihas O Sanskritir Ruprékha (Shillong, 1996).

Chowdhury, Kamilya, Mihir : Banglār Narisanskriti (Kolkata, 1993).

—Anchalik Devata Loksanskriti (Bardhaman, 1992).

Dam, Mrinalkanti, Pal, Nripendranath : Cochbeharér Kavi Dwija Madhabchandra Birachita Chandikar Bratakatha.

Das, Binod Shankar; Roy, Pranab Ed. : Medinipur Itihas O Sanskritir Bibartan (Kolkata, 1989).

Das, Jogesh : Asamer Lokasanskriti (Delhi, 1983).

Das, Krishnaram : Sasthi Mangal (Kolkata, 1333); Granthabali (Calcutta University, 1958).

Das, Lochon : Chatanya Mangal Ed. : Bimanbihari Mazumdar and Sukhamoy Mudhopadhyaya, (Kolkata, 1971).

Das, Purna Chandra : Kanthir Lokachar (Kolkata, 1978).

De, Bela : Brata Chhara Alpana (Kolkata, Pushtakalaya, 1965).

Deb, Chittaranjan : Banglār Lokasahityé Narir Daan (Kolkata, 1990); Banglār Lok Gitakatha (Kolkata, 1986).

Deb, Narayan : Padma-Puran (Ed. Tamanosh Chandra Dasgupta, Kolkata, 1947).

Gangopadhyaya, Kalyankumar : Banglār Lokashilpa (Kolkata, 1368).

Ganguly, Manikram : Dharma Mangal (Edited by Bijitkumar Dutta and Sunanda Dutta, Kolkata, 1960).

Ghosh, Binoy : Banglar Lokasanskritir Samajtattva (Kolkata, 1396).

—Pashchim Banger Sanskriti, First Volume : (Kolkata, 1989).

—Pashchim Banger Sanskriti, Second Volume (Kolkata, 1992).

—Pashchim Banger Sanskriti, Third Volume (Kolkata, 1980).

—Pashchim Banger Sanskriti, Fourth Volume (Kolkata, 1986).

Ghosh, Deviprasad : Baramasi Gaan O Anyanya/Adwaitya Mallabarman (Kolkata, 1990).

Guin, Mrityunjoy : Prachin Bangla Sahitye Lokachar O Lokabiswas (Kolkata, 1992).

Gupta, Bijoy : Padma Puran (Edited by Jayanta Kumar Dasgupta, Kolkata, 1962).

Gupta, Rampran : Bratamala (Kolkata, 1320).

Huq, Khondakar Riazul : Bangladesher Utsav (Dhaka, 1995).

Islam, Sirajul Edited : Bangladesher Itihas (Third Volume, Dhaka, 1993).

Kamalini Sahitya Mandir : Bratadarpan (Calcutta, 1333).

Karan, Sudhirkumar : Shimanta Banglar Lokayan (Kolkata, 1402).

Kathiababa, Sri 108 : Swami Dhananjoydasji Saddharmatattwadip (Kolkata, 1396).

Kavikankan Chandi (Ed, Srikumar Bandopadhyaya and Biswapati Chowdhury, Calcutta, 1974).

Kaviraj, Krishnadas : Sri Sri Chaitanya Charitamrita, Adilila (Edited by Radhagobinda Nath, Kolkata, Fourth Edition).

Khan, Hafiz Rashid Edited : Bangladesher Upajati O Adivasi : Angshidwarityer Natun Dwiganta (Dhaka 1993).

Khan, Shamsuzzaman Edited : Chandrakumar Dey Agranthita Rachana (Dhaka, 1994).

Kiranbala Dasi : Bratakatha (Kolkata, 1319).

Kundu, Kanai : Manasamangal (Calcutta University 1949).

—First Part (Edited by Bijanbehari Bhattacharya Kolkata, 1977).

Mahato, Binoy : Lokayata Jharkhand (Kolkata, 1984).

Maiti, Prodyot Kumar : Samaj O Sanskritir Ruparekha (Midnapore, 1995).

Mamum, Muntasir : Bangladesher Utsav (Dhaka, 1994).

Mazumdar, Asutosh : Meyeder Bratakatha (Kolkata, 1992).

Mazumdar, Dibyajyoti : Bangla Lokkathar Type O Motif Index (Kolkata, 1993).

Mazumdar, Sisir : Uttar banglar Loka Samaj (Kolkata, 1997).

Mitra Mazumdar, Dakshinranjan : Dakshinaranjan Rachanabali (Vol. 1, Kolkata, 1386).

Mitra, Ashok Ed. : Pashchim Banger Puja Parvana O Mela (Vols. 1-5, Kolkata, 1992).

Mitra, Sanat Kumar Ed. : Meyeli Bratabishaye (Kolkata, 1995).

Mukhopadhyaya, Asutosh : Nitya Puja Padhati (Kolkata, 1359).

—Meyeder Bratakatha (Kolkata, 1338).

Mukhopadhyaya, Sunit Kumar : Mela O Utsaver Darpane Banglar Loka Sahitya (Kolkata, 1997).

Murtaja, Dewan Golam : Lokayat Pal-Parvana (Dhaka, 1988).

Pipilai, Bipradas : Manasa Vijaya (Ed. Sukumar Sen, Kolkata, 1980).

Roy, Amarendra : Bangalir Puja Parban (Kolkata, 1356).

Roy, Kaminimukar : Loukik Sabdakosh (Vol. I, Kolkata, 1977 and Vol. II, 1971).

—Banglar Lokadevata O Lokachar (Kolkata, 1980).

Roy, Niharranjan : Bangalir Itihas (Adiparva, Kolkata, 1400).

Roy, Parameshprasaana : Meyeli Brata O Katha (Kolkata, 1315).

Roy, Vidyanidhi, Jogesh Chandra : Puja Parvan (Kolkata, 1390).

Sarkar Swarochish Ed. : Bangla Academy Baisakhi Loka Utsav Prabandha (Dhaka, 1993).

Sarkar, Pabitra : Lokasanskritir Nandantwatta (Kolkata, 1996).

Sarkar, Sukhamoy : Utsaver Utsa (Bihar, 1987).

Sen, Gopikanath : Paschim Banger Lokasanskriti O Sahitya Prasanga (Kolkata, 1394).

Sengupta, Pallav : Puja Parbaner Utsakatha (Kolkata, 1990).

—Loka Sanskritir Simana O Swarup (Kolkata, 1995).

Siddiqui Ashraf : Loka Sahitya (Vol. I, Dhaka, 1994).

Sinha, Pranab Kumar : Prachin O Madhyuger Sahitye Bangali Samaj O Sanskriti (Bankura, 1985).

Suhasini Debi : Meyeli Bratakatha (Kolkata, 1392).

Sur, Atul : Banglar Samajik Itihas (Kolkata, 1982); Bangali Jibaner Nritwattik Roop (Kolkata, 1992); Bharater Nritwattik Parichaya (Kolkata, 1988).

Swami Normalananda : Baro Mase Tero Parvan Ki O Keno (Kolkata, 1395).

Tantrabibhuti : Manasā Puran (Ed. Asutosh Das, Kolkata, 1980).

Thakur, Abanindranath : Banglār Brata (Kolkata, 1402).

Vidyabinod, Kalikishore and Chowdhury, Suresh : Meyeder Bratakatha (Coll. Kolkata, 1393).

Vidyaratna, Kaliprasanna Ed. : Meyeder Bratakatha (Kolkata, 1341).

Hindi

Dwip Publication : Sri Sukhrabar Bratakatha, Agra, 1992.

Janta, Hariram : Himachal Ki Loka Sanskriti (Delhi, 1986).

Misra, Sitaram : Sampurn Brata Aur Taunhar (Kolkata, 1994).

Pakhroli, Prem : Himachal Ka Janjivan Ebong Asthayan (Himachal Pradesh, 1987).

Rajgaria, Champa Devi : Barha Mahino Ka Taunhar (Kolkata, 1991).

Ruchika Publication : Karhwa Chouth Tahtha Ahoi Athey Bratakatha (New Delhi, 1990).

Tantrik Bahal : Manokamanadayak Brata Ebong Touhar (Delhi, 1995).

Bengali Journals

Bamabodhini : Kartick 1298.

—Aghrayan 1298.

Bangla Academy Patrika : Shravan-Asvin 1369, Dhaka.

Bankura Lokasanskriti : 15th year, Second Number, 1402.

Bharati : Numbers 6, 8, 9, 10, 11, 12, 1315.

—Numbers 1, 3, 6, 1319.

Dhaan—Shalikher Desh: April-June 1997 Dhaka.

Durga Puja Sekal Theke Ekal: 10th Asvin 1393.

Gana Kantha—Folk culture number, Murshidabad, 1985.

Gandiva—Special folk number, September-December 1990.

Gomati—November 1974 to April 1977, Numbers.

Janhabi: Kartick, 1315, 4th year 7th Number.

Loka Sanskriti : Baisakh—Asarh 1397.

Loka Sanskriti Gabeshana : Baisakh—Asarh 1397.

Loka Shruti : Asvin 1397—Chaitra 1397.

Lokasanskriti Gabeshana Bishayak : October-December 1991.

Lokayat : January-March 1994.

Loukik Bangla : January-June 1978, Dhaka.

—June 1997, Dhaka.

Madhuparni : Special Cooch Behar District Number 1396-97.

—Special West Dinajpore District Number 1399.

—Special Darjeeling District Number 1996.

Paschim Banga: New Year number 1401.

Protiva: Shravan 1318, Bhadra 1318, Magh 1318, Chaitra 1357.

Purbadri: First Number 10th year 1989.

Sahitya Parishad Patrika : Additional Number 1312.

—1st Number 1313.

—2nd Number 1333.

Sanbarta : Ist year Ist Number 1994.

Shilalipi : Ed. Bankim Mahato.

Index

K